Studying Law at University

Other titles in this series

Studying Science at University
Clare Rhoden and Robyn Starkey

Studying Law at University

Everything you need to know

Simon Chesterman
and Clare Rhoden

ALLEN & UNWIN

Copyright © Simon Chesterman and Clare Rhoden, 1999

Produced by the University of Melbourne through its Learning Skills Unit.

All rights reserved. No part of this book may be reproduced or transmitted in any form or by any means, electronic or mechanical, including photocopying, recording or by any information storage and retrieval system, without prior permission in writing from the publisher.

First published in 1999 by
Allen & Unwin
9 Atchison Street
St Leonards NSW 1590
Australia
Phone: (61 2) 8425 0100
Fax: (61 2) 9906 2218
E-mail: frontdesk@allen-unwin.com.au
URL: http://www.allen-unwin.com.au

National Library of Australia
Cataloguing-in-Publication entry:

Chesterman, Simon.
  Studying law at university: everything you need to know.

  ISBN 1 86448 803 4.

  1. Law—Study and teaching—Australia. 2. Law students—Australia—Handbooks, manuals, etc. I. Roden, Clare. II. Title.

340.071194

Set in 10.5/12 pt Garamond by Bookhouse Digital, Sydney
Printed and bound by SRM Production Services, Malaysia

10 9 8 7 6 5 4 3 2 1

FOREWORD

Competitive entrance requirements mean that students who gain entrance to a Law faculty are excellent students. Unfortunately, school success does not always translate so readily into tertiary success, and university law courses bring quite a new set of challenges—new skills, new vocabulary and a culture all of their own. This book aims to help students develop the special skills they need to succeed in a law course at university.

Simon Chesterman is that rare being, a very successful student who can impart his learning experiences to others in a way that acknowledges the unique set of skills that each individual brings to the task. Simon's own experience as a student is very current: he has recently completed his combined Arts/Law degree (with first-class honours in both Law and Arts) at the University of Melbourne and was awarded a Rhodes Scholarship to undertake postgraduate studies at Oxford. In this book, he teams up with Clare Rhoden, the Senior Academic Skills Adviser at the University of Melbourne's Learning Skills Unit, to demystify the secrets of success in studying law. Clare's refreshingly energetic approach to learning stimulates and captivates young people, and she builds on many years experience working with students to develop their skills and optimise their chances of success.

Studying law requires a unique set of personal, organisational and communication skills, and in *Studying Law at University*, Simon and Clare provide a practical and immensely readable guide to surviving (and enjoying!) your law course.

Patricia McLean
Manager, Equity and Learning Programs
University of Melbourne

CONTENTS

Foreword v
Figures x
Acknowledgments xi
Introduction xii
    Welcome to law xii
    Using this book xiv

Part I Surviving law

1 Why are you studying law? 3
    Why am I here? 3
    Where am I going? 5
    Private practice—the law firms 6
    Public practice—government law 9
    Courtroom dramas 11
    Non-legal work 12
    Combined degrees 13
    Structuring your degree and preparing for employment 15

2 Coping at university 18
    Coping with other students 18
    Female students 20
    Coping with the study 21

STUDYING LAW AT UNIVERSITY

3 Essential study skills: time management 24
   Time management 24
   How to get organised 28
   Your study timetable 30
   Making best use of study time 32
   A further discussion of procrastination 37

4 Essential study skills: reading, notetaking and learning legal concepts 41
   Reading 41
   Tips for reading legal texts 44
   Notetaking 46
   Learning and understanding legal theory 51
   Take some time to explore your study self 54
   Becoming an active learner 56
   Ideas for collaborative learning 58
   Taking advantage of the way memory works 59

Part II Understanding law

5 Crucial concepts 63
   'Law'—a rose by any other name still has thorns 64
   Language is power 67

6 Reading case law 68
   Before you turn a page... 69
   OK, now turn a few pages... 71
   Skim, read, note and review 75

7 Introducing legal theory 78
   What is theory? 78
   How much do I have to know? 79
   Some levels of analysis 79
   Applying the theories 86
   More study hints 87

CONTENTS

Part III Using the law

8 *Writing law essays*	91
Essay writing: the basics	92
Research for your essay	93
Writing your essay	97
Citing authority	98
Using footnotes	100
A postscript—the computer age	104
9 *Preparing for law exams*	106
What is being tested?	106
Open book exams	107
Exam-friendly notes	109
Getting an overview	110
Training for the event	111
Learn to use the law	114
10 *Sitting law exams*	116
Divide and conquer	116
Exam paragraphs—are they helpful?	124
Filling in the gaps	127
Don't panic!	128
What next?	129
11 *Dealing with problems*	130
The bottom line	137

Part IV Conclusion

12 *Final reflections on law*	141
Appendix I: Suggestions for further reading	143
Appendix II: Learning styles quiz	145
Appendix III: A starting point for using web resources	150
Appendix IV: The view from the kitchen	153

FIGURES

3.1	A blank timetable	31
3.2	Example timetable of classes for a combined Arts/Law first-year course	33
3.3	A comprehensive weekly timetable for combined Arts/Law	34
3.4	Example timetable of classes for a combined Law/Commerce first-year course	35
3.5	A comprehensive weekly timetable for combined Law/Commerce	36
6.1	Schematic representation of a case's facts	74
6.2	Sample notes: who, what, where, how, why	77
8.1	Example abbreviations and full citations	104
9.1	Concepts to be considered with regard to 'duty'	110
9.2	Sample exam study notes on the topic of 'duty'	112
10.1	Example time schedule for two hour exam starting at 2.15p.m. with 30 minutes reading time	117
10.2	Characters in a negligence case	121
10.3	Some remedies to consider in Property Law	121
10.4	Some causes of action in Constitutional and Administrative Law	122
10.5	A basic structure for discussing a hypothetical	124
10.6	A basic plan for an exam paragraph on negligence	125
10.7	A more detailed exam paragraph on negligence	125
10.8	An exam paragraph on a contested area of law	126

ACKNOWLEDGMENTS

We would like to thank a number of people who helped us with this project: the Manager of Equity and Learning Programs at the University of Melbourne, Patricia McLean, for her invaluable advice and encouragement, and for giving us the time to get our ideas together and write this work; Ian Malkin for his comments and advice; the faculty staff in Law and Commerce at the University of Melbourne; and our colleagues at the Learning Skills Unit, particularly Aveline Pérez and Robyn Starkey for their sterling work on the timetables in this book and unfailing readiness to answer frantic requests for reading and comments, and Ian Caudwell for his valuable input. We would also like to express our appreciation to the many law students at the University of Melbourne whose experiences are the basis for much of the information in this book. In addition, we would like to thank our publisher, Elizabeth Weiss, for her patience and good humour, always ready at the other end of the e-mail link; and Glenda Harvey of the University's Solicitor's Office for expediting the arrangements for publication and saving us much frustration. Finally, our thanks to Gwyn Lindsay for her time and care over our manuscript as well as for her ready encouragement and support.

INTRODUCTION

> When I started law, it was like entering some bizarre cult. Everyone spoke a private language, they had these obscure rites and rituals—there were even high priests who got about in long black robes with wigs made out of horse-hair!
>
> Future Supreme Court Judge

WELCOME TO LAW

Why this book will help you

Studying law can be a confronting business. Even though the law touches most aspects of our lives, its concepts and institutions often remain mysterious.

For many students who choose to study law, the reality of law school is quite different from their expectations. It is a far cry from the world of smooth-talking lawyers who grace American television programs. In fact the study of law

INTRODUCTION

is an initiation into the peculiar world of rules and procedures that has been evolving over the last thousand or so years. To get the most out of your studies, you need to come to terms with that history, to understand the way legal knowledge is created and used, and to learn how to use the law yourself. Most importantly, you will need to learn the skills of reading, writing and thinking about law. You will need to develop these skills differently from the way you have used reading, writing, and thinking before. Studying at university is very different from studying at high school (see Chapter 2, 'Coping at university'). On top of that, studying law is different from studying other disciplines.

Many students who are offered a place in law at university are high achievers who have done very well in their previous studies. However, often they discover on arrival at university that the demands of the law course are very different from anything they have done before. They may find that the study strategies they rely on are not quite so successful at tertiary level. Other students coming from widely varied backgrounds may be unsure about how to approach the study tasks of the course. In this book, we will help you understand the specifics of studying at university and equip you with strategies for success. You will find that there is more to being at university than studying for exams.

Studying Law at University will teach you the special skills need to succeed in your law course at university. It will also make the world of law less mysterious, so that your studies will be more rewarding and you will be able to realise your full potential when it comes to assessment. This book is designed primarily for first and second year law students, but it will be of use to any student who needs to analyse legal concepts (that is, the ideas behind and around legislation, rather than legislation itself).

STUDYING LAW AT UNIVERSITY

USING THIS BOOK

How this book will help you

This book is divided into three parts.

In Part I, 'Surviving law', we begin by looking at why people decide to study law, the types of jobs it leads to, different ways of structuring degrees and the sorts of courses law offers you. We will then talk about some of the basic skills you need to develop in order to stay on top of your studies and get the most out of your degree.

In Part II, 'Understanding law', we begin demystifying law by introducing you to some of its crucial concepts. Then we turn to one of the most important skills you will need to acquire: reading and understanding the decisions of judges. Third, we discuss legal theory and different ways in which you can develop a more critical understanding of the law.

In Part III, 'Using law', we look at how to apply the skills developed in Part II. The focus is on some of the different ways in which law is assessed at university. While you will find that each institution assesses its students slightly differently, most assessment is by essay and exam, often 'open book' exams. In this part, we look first at writing essays in law—from researching the basic material to formatting the footnotes. Then we show you how best to prepare notes during the year, making sure that your notes summarise the important principles of the course and are 'exam-friendly'. Third, we look at what you should do when you are sitting the exam itself and answering hypothetical problems that challenge you to apply the law that you have studied to an entirely novel situation. Finally, we give you some hints about what to do when (if) things go wrong with your studies.

Throughout the book, the emphasis is on providing practical advice that will help you make the most of your time and your work. You will find that the study of law

INTRODUCTION

gives you plenty of interesting matter to think about. We trust that this book will help you to enjoy the experience as well.

> If, then, an occupier is not liable for the escape of an animal, is he [sic] to be held liable for that of an infant, who from the standpoint of reasoning powers is much the same as a sheep or any other domestic animal?
> *Carmarthenshire CC v Lewis* [1955] AC 549, 560
> (Lord Goddard)

Part I
SURVIVING LAW

WHY ARE YOU STUDYING LAW?

> In the first week of my first year of law school, everyone wanted to know why everyone else decided to study law. It became a sort of running joke to say, 'Well, you know, I got the marks'.
>
> Future Attorney-General

WHY AM I HERE?

'Out of the frying pan ...'

There are many reasons why you might choose to study law. Some students are attracted to understanding the forces that shape our society; others enjoy the thought of getting their hands on those forces. Some students see law as a useful tool for justice, others see it as a respectable and rewarding career. Still others are following the footsteps of family, friends or other people they admire.

But we also know that a great many law students have no definite reason for commencing law. In addition, the reasons given by the rest often change over the course of the degree, as they gain greater understanding of what the law is, what it means, and what it can (and can't) do.

A former Australian Vice-Chancellor recently described Law as having become a de facto Arts degree. By this, he meant that it is now a generalist degree that students

STUDYING LAW AT UNIVERSITY

undertake, not in order to become lawyers but to acquire useful skills that can be applied in a variety of circumstances.

You will understand this when you realise that the material you study while you're at university will almost certainly change from the time you start your studies to the time when you may come to practise law. This means that memorising the substance of the law that you study is less important than you may think. Your main task is understanding the principles of the law and developing the skills to update your knowledge continually and apply existing law to new situations. In fact, the real focus of your studies is the acquisition of these skills, which we list below:

- critical and analytical skills
- the ability to argue clearly and logically
- written and oral presentation skills
- research skills—increasingly using information technology, and
- the ability to understand complex policy issues.

Once you see the study of law as developing a set of skills—rather than grooming you for legal practice—the possibilities for applying it in later life expand considerably. The study of law enables you to use the law, not to recite it by heart. You will learn to appreciate the differences in interpretations and applications, and understand how and why changes occur. You will learn the skills to continue learning about and using the law.

head in the case

WHY ARE YOU STUDYING LAW

WHERE AM I GOING?

'The road less travelled ...'

Two roads diverged in a wood, and I—
I took the one less travelled by ...

Robert Frost

Many law students realise that there are currently more people studying law than practising it. Therefore simple mathematics reveals that either the amount of legal work available will have to increase exponentially, or that not everyone studying law will become a 'lawyer' as such.

Not surprisingly, many law graduates are already moving into fields other than working in a law firm or at the Bar. In this section, we consider some of the different career paths followed by law graduates.

One of the reasons for the great diversity in eventual careers is that many law students these days study law as part of a double degree course.

Cross-check: *The choice and relevance of your second degree is considered in 'Combined degrees'.*

The following discussion of career choices is by no means an exhaustive list. Most universities have careers officers whose purpose is to help you find a job—they will have far more detailed material than can be presented here.

> Note that in most jurisdictions there is a distinction between graduating from law and admission to practice. In some places, such as New South Wales, you must undertake an extra year of study at a law college. In others, such as Victoria, you must complete a certain period of 'articles' (a sort of legal apprenticeship). Ensure

> that you check that you are taking the appropriate subjects to complete your degree and be admitted to practice.

PRIVATE PRACTICE—THE LAW FIRMS

Corporate law firms

Work in a corporate law firm is often presented as the natural consequence of a law degree. Corporate law firms are the ones that sponsor activities in many law schools and whose activities seem to dominate most courtrooms. Although work in a large firm for corporate clients is not for everyone, there is a wide range of opportunities. For example, you could work advising corporations on their business dealings or spend your time litigating their mistakes; you could be employed overseeing public floats on the stock exchange or protecting intellectual property rights and superannuation funds.

Increasingly, many corporate law firms are aiming to provide a 'one-stop shop' for their clients, combining legal and business advice. Of course, the other side of this coin is the growing tendency for larger accounting firms to enter legal practice, meaning work for law graduates in accounting firms. The current trend of privatisation has also increased the work available in areas such as representing governments and developers.

Labour law firms

These are commonly seen as the ideological opposite of the corporate law firms. Law firms dealing with labour laws are firms that primarily represent unions, workers or individuals. As well as industrial/employment relations, these firms may also do personal injury work, insurance, trade practices and more.

The Verdict

Criminal law

When most non-lawyers think of law, they probably think of criminal law first. Criminal law—whether you prosecute or defend—is often seen as the most challenging and rewarding area of law. You may be attracted to this because it can show you cases and situations that are always new and different and challenging, or you might like the idea of confronting the diverse forces of power in our society.

And Justice For All
Murder One

Family law firms

Family law, like criminal law, operates directly at the individual level of human society. Requiring interpersonal skills quite different from other areas of law, family law covers all aspects of marriage and the breakdown of relationships, maintenance and property settlements, and issues relating to the custody and welfare of children.

Kramer versus Kramer
LA Law

Other opportunities

Many law firms are becoming more flexible in their employment practices and it may be possible to vary your employment by:
- going on secondment, where the firm sends you to a client in order to gain experience and to understand that client's needs better, or
- being transferred abroad to another office of the law firm, or to an associated law firm.

Other 'private' work

There is an increasing need for law graduates to work in privatised or semi-government authorities and organisations such as hospitals and educational settings. Universities and

WHY ARE YOU STUDYING LAW

colleges may employ their own legal representatives, and many private schools, for example, use lawyers to conduct much of their business.

Chicago Hope

PUBLIC PRACTICE—GOVERNMENT LAW

Government solicitor

Usually part of the Attorney-General's department, organisations such as the Australian Government Solicitor have much in common with the larger law firms, but with a considerably different area of practice. Lawyers in such an organisation will deal with taxation, customs, migration, freedom of information and conveyancing issues, to name just a few.

The X-Files

Office of Public Prosecutions (or equivalent)

In most jurisdictions, all indictable (more serious) offences are controlled by a centralised office. Work for such an office comprises all aspects of bringing an alleged criminal to trial, from the exercise of the discretion to prosecute to plea-bargaining, from organising witnesses to attending the trial.

Presumed Innocent

Foreign affairs

Although there are traditionally thousands of applicants for a handful of jobs, the prospects of foreign travel and involvement in issues of international significance is a strong attraction for many graduates. The legal office in such departments is usually small, but offers tantalising possibilities in such fields as outer space and nuclear law, through to international trade and economic law.

007

Other government departments

Depending on the jurisdiction, it may be possible to get work as a legal adviser to a committee or department of parliament. This involves scrutinising Bills before they are put to the legislature, as well as legal and policy research. Alternatively, you could consider work for other departments, from the taxation office to the equal opportunity office.

WHY ARE YOU STUDYING LAW

The Pelican Brief

COURTROOM DRAMAS

The Bar—becoming a barrister

Often seen as the 'real' practice of law, being a barrister involves you in the day-to-day working of the courts. Requirements vary in the different jurisdictions, but further study or work experience is commonly required before opening chambers (a barrister's 'shop') and waiting for your first client.

Prior to going to the Bar, it is quite common to work for a few years at a law firm in your area of choice to gain experience and contacts who will send you work. This last aspect is often crucial, as many jurisdictions require barristers to wait for work to be sent their way rather than touting (advertising) for business. For this reason, starting out on your own will usually represent a large financial commitment at first, but eventually you will enjoy a level of independence rarely possible within a law firm.

Virtually all judges are appointed from the ranks of barristers, and barristers are also commonly appointed to appeal tribunals.

Rumpole of the Bailey

Judge's associate

If you want to know about life in court, but you don't want to wait until you're a barrister, and you feel awkward lurking about the cloistered halls, you may consider becoming a judge's associate. This is a position that may vary from being a ghost writer and researcher for a judge to being a personal organiser for a globe-trotting jurist. It provides a unique insight into the workings of the law from a judge's perspective and, as it is usually for a limited time, is often a useful way of investigating a possible move to the Bar.

Dark Justice

NON-LEGAL WORK

Management and administration

Law graduates are increasingly involved more generally in management. These careers range from the management of consulting firms (assisting client companies to expand business opportunities and reduce costs) to moving directly into an administrative position in a particular business.

The Hudsucker Proxy

Academia

Some students can never get enough of law school and come back to teach—often after some years of practice. As a teacher, your activities will spread over a number of areas, including teaching and administration as well as research and writing. One of the major attractions of a career in academia is that it gives you the freedom to pursue your particular area of interest, and may enable you to get involved in public debates (and legal actions) on issues that are more rewarding socially than financially.

Reversal of Fortune

Other

Of course there are many other employment opportunities. Careers where the skills acquired during your law degree may come in useful include: research, journalism, stock-broking and many others. We know law graduates who are now working in medicine, in the popular media such as radio and television, as agents for famous people, and with large sporting organisations and clubs. We also know a couple who are now in politics, one who is very involved in the trade union movement, one who works as a learning or study skills adviser, and quite a few with their own private businesses other than law (one is a winemaker).

COMBINED DEGREES

More than one string to your bow

Because law can lead to such diverse career paths, students are encouraged to combine their studies in law with another degree. This has traditionally seen students studying Arts or Commerce/Economics. In recent years this has expanded somewhat, with Law/Science becoming increasingly popular (with many opportunities emerging in intellectual property and information technology) and the emergence of Law/Engineering and Law/Medicine. About half of all law students will be undertaking combined courses.

The choice of degree is important, and should be based on a balance of

- what you are interested in
- what you think you will do well in, and
- what you think will help you get where you want to go after your studies.

It is essential not to treat your 'other' degree as of secondary importance. Another degree is not merely there to make your life appear more interesting; it expands your areas of expertise and enables you to develop another aspect of your personality, as well as showing you how to think about things in different ways. You may find that at some times, the demands of law and of your other degree compete alarmingly; part of the benefit of this is that it will help you develop the truly professional skills of organising your time and juggling demands on your time. If you are successful at managing these problems, you will have the skills you need to operate in a busy organisation, whichever career you choose.

These are ideas that you can keep in mind whenever you are tempted to think that the second degree's subjects are just wasting your time. This is particularly true of the Arts degree, which may sometimes appear to have little relevance to your career. However, the research, analytical and writing skills that Arts develops will add depth to your studies in law and better equip you to approach new problems in an original way. There are some academics who argue that no-one who works with people on a regular basis can do so successfully without the mind-broadening

WHY ARE YOU STUDYING LAW

experience of an Arts degree. Whatever your second degree it will have benefits for you that will, in the long run, outweigh the difficulties.

Remember that there will be people on campus who can help you with managing your time and your study, especially in the early years when you're just getting the hang of university life. You can make some good contacts through your law students' society, or there may be good on-campus mentor schemes running. There will be advisers in your faculty or department, and there are also learning skills advisers whose brief it is to help you get the most out of your studies. These support people can give you a real boost during demanding times.

> **Cross-check:** *Balancing your study time will be considered in Chapter 3.*

STRUCTURING YOUR DEGREE AND PREPARING FOR EMPLOYMENT

'Youth is wasted on the young'

Breaking up your law degree: time out

It is quite common for law students to break up their studies. Many courses allow leaves of absence: check the rules at your institution for your specific course. A year of doing something else may help you to get your head together and return to finish off your degree(s). Alternatively, some students take a year off between completing their studies and commencing employment (which may have been finalised).

In addition to travel or non-legal work, you may wish to consider varying your studies to:

- complete a year of honours in your other degree, or

- take part in an exchange program to study law or your other degree overseas.

Subject to your personal finances, don't worry that you are delaying employment by a year: the law firms can wait, and are usually more interested in well-rounded individuals than fast-track graduates. (There are, of course, limits to this: don't go to an interview and tell them of your boundless wanderlust!)

Summer and winter clerkships

A brief stint working at a law firm is a great way to see if you want to work in that environment, or at that firm in particular. It also gives the firm a chance to look more closely at you. (In fact, when it comes to permanent employment, some firms will only interview graduates who have taken part in a clerkship program.)

Competition for the relatively few positions being offered is extremely fierce, however. Ask later-year law students what you should expect: in which years of your degree you should apply, and which firms you may be interested in. Note that many organisations other than law firms will also accept students for temporary or part-time work.

Cross-check: *Have another look at the list of career options we gave above.*

If you are accepted for a clerkship, do remember that three four-week clerkships tend to devour your summer holidays (and that the more you accept, the fewer there are to go around).

Applying for employment

It is common for law firms to accept applications from students for employment prior to the completion of their law degrees. These employment opportunities may be subject to guidelines and are usually not available before your final year has commenced. (These guidelines were developed to stop law firms offering jobs to eighteen-year-olds at the end of the first year of a five-year double degree.)

Inquire at your law students' society or the university's career office for more information.

2 COPING AT UNIVERSITY

> The first thing we do, let's kill all the lawyers.
> Shakespeare, *Henry VI*, Part 2

COPING WITH OTHER STUDENTS

> *'Which school did you go to?'*

Even today, in Australia the vast majority of judges are white, middle-class, private school-educated men. This is mostly because of the environment and the time in which they were educated. While law faculties have been traditionally dominated by white, middle-class, private school-educated male students, the mix of students is slowly changing. Since the 1970s in particular, for example, the number of women studying law has increased dramatically, and many law schools now have a majority of female students.

Nevertheless, law schools can be confronting places to enter for a variety of reasons. Some of you will find the high proportion of students who come directly from private schools a bit daunting, especially if they all seem to know each other and appear to have 'private' clubs. At times these students may give you the impression that law students from different backgrounds (such as state high school students, those from more varied ethnic backgrounds, female students, special entry or mature age students) are somehow peripheral to the workings of the law school. You might feel this particularly acutely in the first year of university, when many students will continue to associate in groups of people that they knew from school, or from a similar background. Changes are happening, however, and the student body across all faculties, including law, is now more diverse (and interesting). Rest assured that many students feel isolated and new whatever their background, and that there are many ways to meet people at uni.

You may find it difficult to get to know people at first, because the class sizes are large, and also the teaching staff—tutors and lecturers—seem less approachable than your teachers at school. At first it will be impossible to recognise more than a few fellow students. However, we know that many students make friends on their very first day at university with the person who happens to sit next to them in the first class, and that they stay friends for life. You might feel that 'everyone else has friends and knows where to go and what to do'—many first-year students think this—but the reality is different. Most of them are feeling equally shy and lost. In general, you will do a lot better and make friends more quickly if you take the chance of starting up a conversation with another student at the first opportunity. Sometimes it's as simple as asking the people who sit near you if they would like to have a coffee or a beer after class (depending on the time of day!).

Remember, if you end up feeling isolated, that you are not alone. No matter what size your law school is, all the students have been thrust into a new environment. For many of them, that will involve taking a different path to the one chosen by their close friends from school; others have not come directly from school at all. However, most campuses have clubs and societies that you can join and activities you can get involved in. Many of these will be publicised through

STUDYING LAW AT UNIVERSITY

special activities in Orientation Week, so make sure you attend a couple of these O-Week functions.

The second thing to remember is that, as time passes, groups of friends will inevitably change. Those students who mix only with their old friends will eventually open up to meet new people. And if they don't, they're missing out on one of the real highlights of university: getting to know a whole range of different people in a stimulating environment.

So the message is: keep an open mind and get involved!

FEMALE STUDENTS

Law can be particularly intriguing for women students. This is the case even in the many law schools where female students are in the majority. Many of the issues discussed in law have special significance for women, and the way in which generations of men have chosen to deal with these issues can foster an awkward or oppressive environment. Women continue to be under-represented in the profession, and many theorists argue that law still perpetuates women's social and economic inequality.

If you feel that the way in which lectures or discussions are conducted is inappropriate, raise the issue with other students, the teacher concerned or another teacher that you know, or consult your women's officer or the equal opportunity officer on campus. Things can only change if people draw attention to them and make a concerted effort to bring about change. This is one of the many interesting, stimulating and challenging aspects of studying at university.

Cross-check: *For further discussion of feminist and other critiques of the law, see Chapter 7, 'Introducing legal theory'.*

COPING WITH THE STUDY

'Big fish, big pond'

Given the high entry requirements to study law, many of the students who come to study it have excellent academic records. It is therefore a shock to some of them that they may no longer get the same excellent results when they make the transition from school to university.

The study of law at university is completely different even from legal studies at secondary school. For one thing, there is far less supervision than at school. Lecturers and tutors won't chase you to see how much work you're doing; it's not even certain that they'll dictate exactly what work you should be doing. Lecturers and tutors will talk to students and do their best to be available to answer questions, but because there are so many students, they can have difficulty meeting the demand. (Keep in mind that they have their own research as well as classes across the whole course, and maybe other consultative responsibilities as well.) While it's a good idea to speak up and make yourself known to your teachers at university, you can't rely on them for day-to-day help with your studies. It's up to you to set your own study regime and to keep up with the material.

Remember though that most universities have a learning or study skills adviser or some type of student services officer, and that these people can help you get organised. Of course, the advice in this book will help you address many difficulties.

Another factor that may confuse you is the comparative lack of feedback. It can be very difficult to tell how well you are going in your studies. Comparing your own study routine with that of other students may help, but students are notoriously inaccurate in reporting how much study they do: some of them wildly overestimate to demonstrate what hard workers they are, while others claim to do no work so they can show how clever they are. You need to find a study regime that suits you: one that you can stick to. You will find that in many university courses there is less emphasis on continuous assessment, and more on examination, than you are accustomed to. Even if you have lots of essays to hand in during the semester, it will probably be a long time before you get any feedback about how you performed. Your tutors and lecturers are presuming that most of your learning is happening through self-study. It is easy to get the impression that your teachers simply don't care, but remember that the point of university is to help you realise your potential as a lifelong learner rather than to tell you what's going to be in the exam.

This lack of supervision may seem like freedom for the first couple of months, but when you realise how short the university year is, and how much more work you have to do compared to when you were at school, you'll appreciate that you need to start early, and to keep working throughout the university year. You can have a good rest over the summer between clerking stints!

Cross-check: *See Chapter 3, 'Essential study skills: time management'.*

It is usually very helpful to be able to talk through issues in the course with other students. Different people get different things out of their studies and bring different life experiences to university: sharing views on the issues you discuss in class is a big part of what tertiary education is all about. More formal study groups may assist you to prepare for end of year exams, while fostering a spirit of camaraderie—you against the law—can help you all to cope. Beware, though, of those students who are too competitive to work collaboratively; everyone in the group must be responsible and committed to the idea of group work.

Steady work throughout the year is your best bet. This doesn't mean that you should become obsessed with working all day, every day; a common problem experienced by law students is that they become fixated on perfection. Because of their high expectations of themselves, they lose the perspective necessary to manage a number of different study commitments at once, and end up focusing on a relatively small task that (they think) must be done perfectly. Sometimes you just have to accept that no one has the perfect understanding of a particular issue and that all you can do is adopt a position on it. In fact, that may be the whole point of studying this issue at university level—that there is no absolute 'right' answer—and this is in fact why the issue is such an interesting one. You will find that what is being tested is rarely whether you get the 'right' answer—what matters is how you justify the position that you do adopt.

3 ESSENTIAL STUDY SKILLS: TIME MANAGEMENT

TIME MANAGEMENT

'Time flies when you're having . . . fun?'

There will always be many things you want to do at university. Balancing your social life with study, and balancing the many extra-curricular activities available with essay and exam commitments, can be a challenge in itself.

It is easy in a course with relatively few 'contact' hours to see these few hours as the total of your academic week. Too often, however, a week or so away from the day an essay is due or an exam is scheduled, students are 'surprised' to discover that they are not prepared. Provided you have nothing else to do that week, you may get through it. But law doesn't have to be such a series of small heart attacks.

In this section, we debunk some of the myths that lead to this happening, and outline some useful strategies for managing your time more effectively.

> **Myth No. 1:** *I work best under pressure.*
> **Translation:** *I can't work unless there's a deadline looming like the sword of Damocles over my head.*

COPING AT UNIVERSITY

Few people genuinely work 'best' under pressure. Instead it is a case of finding it difficult to work at all without that pressure. This is one of the major issues confronted by students who come to university from a highly supervised secondary education; without teachers to hassle you constantly, it is easy to believe that there is no work to be done.

Planning ahead to allocate time in advance of deadlines doesn't mean sacrificing your social life (entirely). It does mean learning that a consistent amount of work throughout the academic year (which, after all, is pretty short) will earn you better results than a few frantic weeks at the end of semester.

In fact, you need to start thinking of yourself as a professional already. It's now totally up to you to balance your study tasks (regular tasks and special assessment-related ones), work if you have it, social activities, family commitments, sport and leisure.

Cross-check: *Look at the timetables in Figures 3.1 to 3.5.*

> The time has come to record some matters. The existence of the motor car in the post-WW II era has been of great value to the legal profession. The recovery of damages for persons injured by the motor car has been, and still is, the largest single source of work available to the profession . . . The stage has been reached where it can be recognised that all sorts of litigation suffer from a lack of professional knowledge, of application, of industry and from the general sloppiness which today marks the typical presentation of this class of action. It is as if the barrister—and the solicitor—do not much heed the result so long as a fair measure of fee-recovery is entailed. Well, for my part, I acknowledge that the motor

> car accident case does not place the greatest professional demand on a barrister or a solicitor but I certainly have now reached the stage when I am no longer prepared to sit and listen silently to cases being incompetently or lazily presented.
>
> *Nazir v Hertz of Australia Pty Ltd* (District Court of NSW, Thorley J, 15 June 1979)

Myth No. 2: *Deadlines just creep up and surprise me.*
Translation: *I don't think about essays or exams until I become overwhelmed by panic (see Myth No. 1).*

Except in the extremely unlikely case where a lecturer actively conceals the due date of an essay, there is no excuse for 'forgetting' that an essay due date is coming up. Some students still cry 'Nobody told me that...' Well, it's up to you to find out what assessments you have and when they are due. Get into the habit of checking noticeboards and reading ALL of your class handouts.

Myth No. 3: *I don't need a draft/plan.*
Translation: *I'm not sure how to go about this essay so I'm putting off starting it.*

It's tempting to tell yourself that you haven't got anything on paper because, well, you have it all worked out in your head and you'll be able to sit down and write the whole assignment on the night before it's due. At university, more than ever you'll find that a professional level of presentation is required, and that's impossible to do without at least one draft and a heap of high quality editing. Just getting the references right can take hours. And that goes double for the content of the essay: you'll need to draft your ideas and responses and work on them to ensure that your essay is well-structured, has good links between and within sections, has a good balance between references and originality, and so on.

> **Cross-check:** *See the discussion about writing law essays in Chapter 8.*

> **Myth No. 4:** *Inspiration will come.*
> **Translation:** *I can't understand the topics and I don't know where to start.*

Perhaps Inspiration will arrive, but it's unlikely that she will come along armed with all the references you should have read in the weeks before the due date. Start your investigations early—you can talk over the topics or the readings with friends or with a lecturer or tutor. You don't need to know exactly what you're going to say in the assignment when you start; it's meant to be a developmental process during which your understanding of the issues and complexities grows along with your ability to discuss them in a well-presented essay.

> **Myth No. 5:** *I'll do it after X.*
> **Translation:** *I'm procrastinating (again).*

Students are the world's best procrastinators: some of them have worked it into an art form. Sometimes it's a sign of confusion about what is involved in the assignment itself, but usually procrastination is a kind of lazy habit. (Reminder: see what Thorley J had to say about incompetence and laziness in the quote earlier in this chapter.) You may have been training yourself to perform only under extreme pressure (see Myth No. 1). There are better ways to live! You could even try doing something *before* X, or making sure X is timetabled sensibly into your week.

Cross-check: *Look at the timetables in Figures 3.1 to 3.5.*

HOW TO GET ORGANISED

'Some tips to avoid the heart attacks ...'

At the start of the year, get a yearly planner and fill in all the deadlines you have for your courses. Mark in the holidays as well to cheer yourself up.

How much work do you need to do in order to succeed at university level? That depends a lot on the kind of worker you are—everyone has different preferences and strengths—but we can give you some broad outlines and suggestions.

Finding time to study

Success at university depends on more than just attending classes. For each hour of class time, most students will need to put in at least an hour of study. (For some subjects, you will need more.) 'Study' in this case means preparing, reading, and reviewing your notes after class. If you have assignments or essays, you will need to budget extra time for them.

All of these study tasks will add up to quite a number of hours. As a rough guide, if you are studying full-time, you should be putting in about 40 hours a week (including classes or *contact hours*). Towards the end of semester, and during swot vac, you may need to spend even more time studying. It sounds rather like a full-time job, doesn't it?

As we said before, the best way to cope is to work steadily. It's important to keep abreast of what is happening in each of your subjects; there is too much in each for you to leave studying until swot vac. You will do better if you organise your study time to occur often, in shorter rather than longer blocks of time.

Instead of procrastinating, get into the DIN (do it now) habit. Keeping up every week is a golden rule of learning at tertiary level. Even if you don't cover all the week's reading before you get something else new, do some work in each subject every week. It isn't necessary for you to know or even understand everything the first week that you encounter it. Trust yourself to take the ideas and issues on board, and keep moving.

On this point, it's important to realise that you're not falling behind everyone else if you don't understand everything as soon as it is presented to you. The ideas and concepts presented in law school are not simple: they're challenging and therefore interesting. Allow yourself space to grow into the new ways of thinking. Trust your own ability to work things out in the long run: if you don't understand the idea at first, just accept it until you know enough to begin challenging it.

Remember that you should look on your (full-time) study as a full-time occupation. You are in fact much like a professional worker doing a 9–5 type of day. This also means that you should take a break for lunch, and for coffee or tea (if you can) at some point. However, you don't have to do all your study between 9 a.m. and 5 p.m. You have a great deal of freedom in how you go about your study, and it's important to use your freedom wisely. You may have moved out of home for the first time, or be staying in one of the university colleges—all this freedom can go to your head. It's now your responsibility to make sure you get your work done.

YOUR STUDY TIMETABLE

Figure 3.1 is an example of a blank timetable. You can photocopy this chart and fill it in to suit your own circumstances, keeping in mind that there is more to life than sitting in law lectures. Note that there are seven days in the study week, not five as some student diaries would lead you to believe.

When you organise your timetable, keep these points in mind:

- Start by filling in all your contact hours (tutes, lectures, seminars).
- Put in all your other commitments (paid work, netball practice, household chores, favourite TV shows).*
- Evaluate the 'spare' time remaining and think about your personal preferences. Be realistic. Don't block out 6:00–8:00 every morning for study if you don't get up till 9:00. Find a couple of hours in each day to use as study time.
- Divide your study times into 30–60 minute blocks.
- Don't just write 'study' in those blocks of time. Indicate for yourself exactly what you should be doing: 'read for HIPOL seminar', 'do commerce problems', 'review lit notes', 'get a time in the computer lab'.
- The odd one or two hour gaps between classes are not necessarily recess. Of course you can have a coffee for half an hour, but use the rest of the time to do a little reading, review some notes or borrow library books. Perhaps do that first, and have a break for the last 30 minutes.
- Include some regular study times for revision and assignment work.

---

* If your timetable looks full at this point, you may need to do a bit of thinking about the number of extra activities you are undertaking—there are many more study-related tasks to go in.

	Monday	Tuesday	Wednesday	Thursday	Friday	Saturday	Sunday
8:00							
9:00							
10:00							
11:00							
12:00							
1:00							
2:00							
3:00							
4:00							
5:00							
6:00							
Evening							

Figure 3.1 A blank timetable

Figure 3.2 is an example of classes that might constitute a first-year Arts-Law student's timetable. However, there are many other activities you need to include in your weekly schedule.

Figure 3.3 is a full timetable which includes activities, work and study times. This student does a number of extra activities, and lives at home with kind parents who don't require her to do many chores. Figures 3.4 and 3.5 show similar timetables for a combined Law/Commerce course.

Even if you aren't a timetable sort of person, it's a good idea to at least *try* using one, and to get into the habit of using your diary so you don't get ambushed by assignment-due dates (see Myth No. 2, above). At the very least, having a timetable makes you aware of what needs to be done regularly.

If the timetable isn't working, then adapt it to your needs and preferences. Don't stick to it no matter what. A good timetable has room to accommodate disasters, and can be flexible. A good law student (or, for that matter, a good lawyer) needs to be able to do the same.

MAKING BEST USE OF STUDY TIME

It is often better to think of your study in terms of tasks, not as stretches of time. It's more productive to say: 'At 11:00 I'll make my own flow chart of the arguments in that road accident case' than to say 'I'd better do some study'. In this way you can also increase your motivation; it feels good to finish a task, but it can be difficult to know when you've done enough 'study'.

It's also wise to keep in mind the old saying about 'all work and no play'. You really need—like a fully professional worker—to create a balanced lifestyle for yourself. If you've honestly done all the work you need to for the day, don't keep sitting at your desk. Have a break, and enjoy it. Go and do the mythical X (see Myth No. 5, above). Chase up

	Monday	Tuesday	Wednesday	Thursday	Friday	Saturday	Sunday
8:00							
9:00		Torts and the Process of Law		Torts and the Process of Law			
10:00	Archeol. 134 Lecture		Archeol. 134 Lecture				
11:00	Crim Justice Tutorial						
12:00	Crim Justice Lecture			Crim Justice Lecture			
1:00	LUNCH	LUNCH	LUNCH	LUNCH			
2:15	History and Philosophy of Law		History and Philosophy of Law				
3:15							
4:15		Archeol. 134 Tutorial					
5:15							
6:00							
Evening							

Figure 3.2 Example timetable of classes for combined Arts/Law first-year course

	Monday	Tuesday	Wednesday	Thursday	Friday	Saturday	Sunday
8:00	**SWIM**		SWIM		SWIM		
9:00	Prep if needed	Torts and the Process of Law	Prep if needed	Torts and the Process of Law	Review		GOLF
10:00	Archeol. 134 Lecture		Archeol. 134 Lecture		Catch up on reading and assignments		
11:00	Criminal Justice Tutorial	Read for Archeol	Read for HPL	Coffee with Giles			
12:00	Criminal Justice Lecture	HPL read and review		Crim Justice Lecture			
1:00	LUNCH	LUNCH with Carl and Sarah	LUNCH (with movie club)	LUNCH	LUNCH		LUNCH
2:15	History and Philosophy of Law		History and Philosophy of Law	Library and Assignment Work			Family
3:15		Library				**WORK**	
4:15	BREAK	Archeol. 134 Tutorial	BREAK	BREAK	**WORK**		Read for Crim Read for HPL
5:15	Read for Torts	**Debating**	Review and read for Torts	More Library			
6:00				**Coaching School Debating**			
Evening	"Friends" Review notes		"X Files" TV		GO OUT	GO OUT	TV and Videos

Figure 3.3 A comprehensive weekly timetable for combined Arts/Law

	Monday	Tuesday	Wednesday	Thursday	Friday	Saturday	Sunday
8:00							
9:00	Micro-economics Lecture		Micro-economics Lecture				
10:00		Quantitative Methods Lecture		Quantitative Methods Lecture			
11:00	History and Philosophy of Law		History and Philosophy of Law				
12:00				Accounting IA Workshop			
1:00	LUNCH	LUNCH	LUNCH (with movie club)	LUNCH			
2:15	Micro Tutorial		Accounting IA Lecture	Accounting IA Lecture			
3:15		Quant. Meth Tutorial	Accounting IA Tutorial				
4:15		Torts and the Process of Law		Torts and the Process of Law			
5:15							
6:00							
Evening							

Figure 3.4 Example timetable of classes for a combined Law/Commerce first-year course

	Monday	Tuesday	Wednesday	Thursday	Friday	Saturday	Sunday
8:00	SWIM		SWIM		SWIM		
9:00	Micro-economics Lecture	Review Micro	Micro-economics Lecture	Accounting tute problems	Catch up Assignments and Library		GOLF
10:00	Micro tute problems/reading	Quantitative Methods Lecture	Coffee with Giles	Quantitative Methods Lecture			
11:00	History and Philosophy of Law	QM tute work with Jane	History and Philosophy of Law	Read and do tute probs for Accounting			
12:00		Library		Accounting IA Workshop	Torts Read/Review	Catch up on Accounting	
1:00	LUNCH	LUNCH	LUNCH	LUNCH	LUNCH		Lunch
2:15	Micro tutorial	Accounting tute problems	Accounting IA Lecture	Accounting IA Lecture			Family
3:15	Read for QM	Quant. Meth Tutorial	Accounting IA Tutorial	BREAK		WORK	
4:15	Read for Torts	Torts and the Process of Law	Library Read for Torts	Torts and the Process of Law	WORK		Read for Micro
5:15	Coaching School Debating	Debating	Read/Reveiw for HPL				Read for HPL
6:00			Accounting review				
Evening			"X Files" catch up	Review QM	GO OUT	GO OUT	TV and videos

Figure 3.5 A comprehensive weekly timetable for a combined Law/Commerce first-year course

those important social contacts, enjoy time with friends and meeting new people.

You need regular exercise to keep healthy. This will help you to avoid the common colds and flu that plague many students. It will also increase your metabolic rate, which is good for your thinking as well as your digestion. For the same reasons, you need a healthy diet and a sensible sleep pattern. If you're doing paid work as well, or just have a very active social life, make sure you don't become too fatigued.

Giving yourself permission not to study (and not to feel guilty) is important, because a rest needs to be a real rest if it is going to refresh you. The key to a successful and fulfilling time at university is a balanced, regular pattern of mixed activities and tasks that helps sustain your interest in life and enables you to continue developing your knowledge base. A lawyer who is completely divorced from the real world will have very little to help him or her relate to clients.

A FURTHER DISCUSSION OF PROCRASTINATION

As we said before, all students are procrastinators. Some are better at managing their problem than others. At the start of semester most of your deadlines seem a long way off, so it may seem reasonable to put off study to play tennis or go to the pub for the afternoon. However, if procrastination about study gets to be a habit, you can find yourself in deep trouble at the end of semester.

The time management ideas we have suggested in this chapter will help you to develop good study habits. The best way to beat procrastination is to do a little bit every day, because the longer you put things off, the harder it is to get going. Remember, motivation is a key to successful study, and you can only stay motivated and interested if you let yourself become mentally involved with the issues you are studying.

If you have difficulty starting your study tasks, you might need to adjust your study environment. Some people find it easier to work where other people are also studying. If you find the atmosphere of hard work in the law library has a good influence on you, then organise to stay at university a bit later (or get in early) and do your work there.

A well-organised study space, one that is organised to suit you, can help to settle you into study mode. Put everything you need on the desk before you sit down, so that you are not tempted to wander around your room looking for things and being distracted. Some people like to play specific study music to help focus their thoughts: they play these pieces each time they work. There are theories, for example, about Baroque music encouraging a studious mindset. You may prefer something else.

You can recruit other people to help you. Explain to the people you live with the level of nagging you need; however, reminders from other people will sometimes just make you more stressed. Collaborative learning can help you get your study habits on track—organise to meet a friend, and make an agreement not to tempt one another to procrastinate. Tutors, lecturers and learning skills advisers can also help you by giving you deadlines to hand in drafts of your work. This strategy not only gets the work done before time, it helps you to improve the final product.

At the end of every study session, make a note of what you were thinking or doing, and leave your books open on your desk (if possible). Lots of procrastination occurs as meandering before you sit down and fidgeting once you have sat down. If you leave yourself something definite to get back to, and a pointer to the important concepts you were thinking about, you will find it easier to take up where you left off. Of course, the more quickly you return to study, the more effective this strategy will be.

Active learning is a big help with time management. Try to have specific goals and interesting ways to accomplish them when you sit down at your desk.

Still looking for more ideas? There is some good online study skills advice available. The Learning Skills Unit at the University of Melbourne <http://www.services.unimelb.edu.au/lsu/> and Unilearning: Learning Resources for University Students <http://www.unilearning.net.au/> are good places to start.

How does time management work in practice? Some good guidelines:

- In your diary (get a diary), mark in the deadlines as well as a few warnings that the deadline is approaching. For example, mark 'three weeks to contracts essay' and note down the tasks to do with that essay that need to be done that week. Completing these tasks will help you get the essay in on time and help you get a better mark. For example, you might write 'two weeks to contracts essay, read and summarise A and B, write draft of section 3' and so on.
- Keep up to date with your notes. Take notes when you read and during class, and try to prepare summaries when you reach the end of a topic. When it comes to exams you will need summaries, and you will find it much easier to make a summary if you do it when the material is fresh in your mind.
- Go to class. Even if you haven't done your reading for a particular class, it is crucial that you stay in touch with what is going on. This is important if only to discover what aspects of the topic are being emphasised or omitted from the course. If you cannot go to a class, ask another student to give you a copy of the notes. However, often you will find that making time to meet for a coffee soon after the class will help you more; you

can learn more about the concepts by talking them over than by trying to decipher someone else's notes.
- Use small amounts of time wisely. If you have set aside time to study, don't think that just because you have less than an hour it is impossible to achieve anything. That is nothing but another convenient myth. There are plenty of small tasks you need to do: continue your reading, summarise a small area that is troubling you, do some photocopying, start your reference list.
- Change tasks. If you find yourself getting frustrated, alternate study tasks, topics or subjects. Have a few different things to go on with: switch between your courses; have one essay that you are planning at the same time as you are finishing another; switch from reading judgments to journal articles; make diagrams or flow charts of the main ideas in the judgments.
- Seek help. Don't give up—if it all seems hopeless, get in touch with a friend, another law student, a learning skills adviser, or a teacher, and talk about it. Above all, don't panic. We talk a little more about what to do when things go wrong in Chapter 11.

4 ESSENTIAL STUDY SKILLS: READING, NOTETAKING, AND LEARNING LEGAL CONCEPTS

> Of making many books there is no end; and much study is a weariness of the flesh.
> *Ecclesiastes* 12:12

To do well in your law studies, you will need to make the most of your study time. This chapter describes how you can improve your reading and notetaking skills and maximise your memory to enhance your learning of legal theory.

READING

> Some books are to be tasted, others to be swallowed, and some few to be chewed and digested.
> Francis Bacon, 1625

While we're fresh on the topic of time management (see Chapter 3), let's consider the task that takes up most of the typical student's (and the typical lawyer's) time: reading. You need to become very good at reading quickly and grasping the main ideas. There is a more detailed discussion of reading case law in Chapter 6, but here we will just give a few hints about reading more quickly. If you are doing a combined degree, as many law students are, you will also have reading for your other course. These suggestions will help with that reading too.

One good way to tackle all the reading you have to do is to develop your skills as a skim reader. You already use this skill every day: when you check the paper for sports results or glance over a menu to find something that interests you. You don't read word-for-word, and yet you manage to extract the information that you want. How can you apply this type of reading to your studies?

Skim-reading

Why are you reading?

You will do a lot of reading. Perhaps most of your study time will be taken up with reading cases, legislation, textbooks, journal articles. So it's essential that you develop the ability to read quickly and to understand what you read.

You need to think about what you are reading, not just to plough through it. Therefore you don't need a photographic memory (see the section 'Learning legal concepts' later in this chapter). Reciting long quotes from judgments only demonstrates that you have a good memory—not that you understand what you have read. Keep in mind that it is your *understanding* that will be tested.

We don't propose to teach you speed-reading (there are a few books on the market about increasing your reading speed). In fact, we are much more interested in efficient reading than in speed-reading. This is because most of your reading at university is for a purpose: it is of no value reading with amazing speed if you don't grasp the major points of the judgments. As we said before, it is your understanding and appreciation of what you read that counts, not how much you read in a given time.

> I took a speed reading course and read *War and Peace* in twenty minutes. It involves Russia.
>
> Woody Allen

This is not to say that you can't improve the speed of your reading. Like all physical activities, reading speed increases with practice. If you have problems reading efficiently, or think you should read more quickly, find out if your student union runs courses on speed-reading, or investigate the study skills unit at your university. They usually have lots of advice on more efficient reading (and some of them have advice online—see Appendix 3). Remember, however, that your goal is quicker *understanding*, not just quicker reading. Have you ever read from the top of one page in your text book to the bottom, but discovered that nothing went in? Your eyes were doing the physical activity, but your brain wasn't moving with them.

So what you really need are some tips to help you get more out of your reading in the same time, or to get the same value from your reading in a shorter time (of course, it would be even better to combine the two—get more out of your reading, *and* do it in a shorter time).

It is possible to learn some shortcuts that will help you understand legal texts (or any study reading) more quickly, and prevent you from wasting time. One important way is to ask yourself questions as you read. Why are you reading this? Is it just to fill in time between classes, or do you expect the article to give you some specific information?

You can read for multiple purposes:

- For an overview of the topic.
  It is important to remain aware of the broad aims of each course. Read the course description carefully. The matters mentioned there are likely to be examined. It is also a good idea to read over the course notes—do this several times during the semester. While you do need to 'learn' many details, you should also always be asking yourself what the implications of each journal article or

case are to the subject as a whole. However, overview reading can be fairly speedy.
- For a context in which to consider the topic.
There is currently an emphasis on critical perspective. Therefore, you may read an article to gain knowledge about a particular critical methodology which you can then apply to a specific case or exercise. While reading, ask yourself: What critical assumptions is this person making? How could this approach be used in the example case? What sort of a way is this to look at the topic? Having asked questions like this, you can then return to the topic with renewed vigour.
- For details of a specific issue or decision.
After reading a case, you may feel that your knowledge of a certain field is limited. If so, you should turn to the textbooks for background information. In this case you will probably read more slowly, with an eye for detail. With your new feel for the background, you can then analyse how the specific case accords with the general principles.
- For the background of an issue or decision.
If you have time, you should try to read some of the other cases referred to in a judgment. Then re-read the original case; you will find this second reading much easier.

Often judges refer to a long line of precedent before coming to a slightly different conclusion. Ask yourself broad questions such as: What assumptions was this line of precedent based on? Why did the Court choose to go a different way?

TIPS FOR READING LEGAL TEXTS

'Fools rush in'

There is almost always an alternative to wading straight into a 200-page judgment, or 100-page Act of Parliament. If you ever get to the point where you've read a few pages and have completely lost track of what's going on, stop and try to think of a better way to approach the text.

One way of improving the amount you get out of your reading is to first have a look at the structure of the piece that you are reading.

If it's a long case, look for the headnote, the brief summary that appears at the start of judgments in the law report volumes.

If the text deals with a particular area of law, consider reading about that area in a textbook or legal encyclopedia (see Chapter 7).

Don't feel compelled to read from beginning to end. Try moving around the text so that you know where it's going. If it's a judgment and it isn't clear where the judge is going with her reasoning, jump to the end so that you know.

Get an overview

Try to develop a 'filter' to work out what is relevant and what is not. Be wary of the judge who spends five pages discussing case law and concludes: 'But of course since the Trade Practices Act, that's all irrelevant now'. Looking at the first and last sentences of each paragraph should give you an idea of where the piece is going.

If a particular section appears less relevant to you, just read enough of it to keep in mind what the judge is talking about while moving quickly through the text. Note that cases (and, to a lesser extent, legislation) often fall within more than one area of law.

Many cases have a 'dissent' (a judge who disagrees with the majority decision). It may sometimes be less important to read these judgments. But if you have time, hearing both sides of a particular issue will usually give you a better understanding of that area of law.

Keep asking questions

> Reading furnishes the mind only with materials of knowledge; it is thinking that makes what we read ours.
>
> John Locke

As you are reading, keep thinking to yourself: Why is this being written? Why is this important? How does this justify the conclusion that follows?

Cross-check: *The particular skills of reading case law are considered in Chapter 6; researching for essays is discussed in Chapter 8.*

NOTETAKING

You will have two major notetaking assignments: taking notes from your reading and taking notes in class. As with reading, you will find that your notetaking will be much more valuable if it has a focus. You need to think about the purpose of the notes. Are you collecting information for an essay? Are you trying to make a record to jog your memory about a case? Are you wanting to get a handle on the lecturer's views of a particular judgment?

Why are you taking notes?

Taking notes usually serves multiple purposes:

- it helps you stay awake and focused on the lecture

- it helps you remember and process material as you are reading or hearing it
- it gives you a basis for essay and assignment writing
- it forms the basis of summaries that you can use for exams, and
- it gives you a record in case you later forget the material.

For most of us, the last purpose is the most important. With that in mind, you should try to ensure that the notes you take are going to be useful.

Notetaking in lectures

> A lecture is where the notes of the professor become the notes of the student without passing through the mind of either one.
>
> Anonymous

Make sure that doesn't happen to you!

Write the topic and date of the lecture at the top, so that you won't have any of those 'where are the notes I took at that class in May that I need right now?' disasters when it comes to essay writing. Remember that in lectures, you can add your own comments to what the lecturer says; you may want to chase up these points later. You shouldn't be trying to write down everything that is said (your main task in lectures is to *understand* what is being said); instead, your notes form a record that jogs your memory and points you to further reading.

Leave lots of space in your notes. This makes it easier to skim over them later, as well as making it possible to return and add comments. Use headings and different levels of indentation from the margin to show how information is grouped under a particular topic. (See the sample notes below.)

Use colours, highlighters, symbols—anything that will help you skim back over the work at a later date. But don't get carried away with colour coding or perfectionism: notes are a perfect example of not judging a book by its cover. If you have beautiful pages of notes but never look at them, you'll have a great deal of trouble putting them to good use in an exam (see Chapters 9 and 10).

Notes taken in class are most useful if you look at them soon after the class—within 24 hours is best (otherwise you might forget what your clever abbreviations mean). Check your notes for legibility, completeness, and links to reading or discussions.

Cross-check: *See 'Learning legal concepts' later in this chapter.*

Remember, too, that the notes that suit others may not suit you. Work to develop a style that you are comfortable with and that is useful to you. Of course you can incorporate others' ideas, but don't try to copy exactly what someone else does—they are not you, and they can't possibly learn in exactly the same way that you do.

What should you write?

Avoid writing unnecessary information—be selective about what you are going to record. Try to work out what is important and how you may use it later on. As a last resort, if you don't understand what the lecturers are saying (and for some reason you are not able to ask them to explain it), just write down as much as you can and talk it over with a friend or look it up in a textbook later.

Try to make a clear distinction between facts and law. Usually, the facts of a particular case are less important than the legal principle it establishes, and they are also easier to remember (because they form a kind of story). Therefore you may only need to write down a few details of the facts, but far more notes on the legal significance of the case. Remember that it is the larger legal context you are studying—the principles and judgments—not the case itself.

Another thing to listen for is when your teacher talks about the course structure—issues that are important, what's examinable and what's not. When that happens, take copious notes.

Cross-check: *The preparation of notes for exams is discussed in Chapter 9.*

Notetaking from reading

Just as you don't want to lose your notes from a lecture, you don't want to find yourself with pages of great information from some text whose name and author you can't remember. So the first thing you do when taking notes from texts is to get down the bibliographic details.

This is essential when you are recording details from a book that you can't photocopy. However, these days much of your reading will be done from photocopies. This has built-in dangers: the rise of the photocopier and the highlight marker as study tools has created specific problems. For one thing, highlighting (or underlining) implies that you will go back and read the text later, when in reality you will often run out of time to have a second look at everything. Second, you will find it difficult to collect all the relevant pieces of paper together when you are drafting an essay, and waste lots of time hunting through your huge bundle of photocopying (of course, you may also discover that the important photocopy has gone mouldy at the bottom of your aerobics bag). Third, you may find that you are not getting the most out of your reading: your mind is occupied with 'will I highlight this bit or not?' rather than with understanding the actual ideas in the text. Taking notes can keep you a little more focused.

Even so, some students say they don't like to take notes, they prefer to underline or highlight the important points. Just remember that highlighting is not the same as understanding, and it is important to be aware of its drawbacks.

It isn't always necessary to take notes when you read, especially if you are reading for context or background. However, notetaking can be an active learning tool.

If you are reading in order to collect material for an assignment you need to write, taking notes in your own words is the first step towards writing a draft. When you sit down to write, these notes are far more useful than pages of highlighted text in someone else's words. Some students can take notes directly onto the computer; this is really useful when it comes to assignment writing.

If you must highlight, be selective, and write your own comments and questions in the margin.

Use efficient reading strategies such as previewing, skimming, and reading with a purpose. Consider limiting your reading time to frequent short periods so that you can stay more focused on the task and complete the material in sensible sections. Sometimes sitting at your desk for hours on end can be mind-numbing, not helpful.

You should be making efforts to become familiar with the material, because the more you know about anything, the easier it is to learn more. You will find that you become much more efficient when you are comfortable with the way law texts are written and with the vocabulary of the specific legal question.

New words and how to cope with them

One factor about reading and notetaking that may be worrying you is the amount of new vocabulary that you are encountering in the texts. You may be tempted to stop at every new word and look it up. There are dangers in this.

One is that when you consult a dictionary (even a dictionary of legal terms), you cannot always make sense of the sentence in front of you. The context has too great an effect on the meaning.

Another problem is that when you keep stopping to look up words, you lose the thread of the information you are reading. So the time you spend looking up words can mean a big delay in understanding the overall concepts of the material.

A different approach is to collect a few new words (in a special notebook or at the bottom of your page) and then have half an hour looking them up when you don't feel motivated enough to do anything more taxing. This means that when you're reading the text, you just keep reading; you will find that many of the words will become clear as you read more about the topic or see the words used in a few different sentences. Of course, if there is only one word that is getting between you and the total meaning, look it up straight away and then continue.

Cross-check: *See Chapter 5, 'Crucial concepts'.*

If you use your reading time wisely, read from a wide range of sources and read often, you will find that you soon become very familiar with the ideas of law and the conventions of legal writing. This familiarity will lead to understanding, which will help you gain good marks, especially in open book exams.

LEARNING AND UNDERSTANDING LEGAL THEORY

Learning theoretical concepts can be challenging, particularly when you have a great many of them thrust at you all at once, or when learning a new concept depends upon your understanding of a previous one about which you don't feel very sure.

It's important to come to grips with theory because theories help lawyers and jurists to organise ideas. Once you understand the principles, other things may fall into place.

Remember that the emphasis is on mental work with the ideas, not merely cramming as many words as possible into your head.

What are you learning this for?

One thing to consider is that your study tasks should reflect not only your motivation and desire to gain a knowledge of the law, but also the type of assessment tasks you will be facing. If you need to write short essays on specific issues in an open book exam, then you should spend some time throughout the semester writing short essays on specific issues. If you need to delineate points of law in a list format, then practise writing lists. If you need to write longer essays about legal concepts for the history of law exam, then practise writing longer essays. In other words, don't just read over the material and hope that some of the information will stick.

Cross-check: *There is more about preparing for and sitting law exams in Chapters 9 and 10.*

We have already talked about organising your time (see Chapter 3) so that you can fit in regular study time throughout the semester. What are some of the tasks that you should be slotting into those couple or more hours every day?

We've talked about reading, and that will take up a great

ESSENTIAL STUDY SKILLS

deal of your study time. In the next section, we're going to talk about how to get the best value from your study time.

Feeling overburdened with work and a little confused is a common problem for first year students. Partly that's because of issues such as the amount of material you need to cover, the quick pace of delivery, the large class sizes and the lack of individual supervision. But you can learn to adapt to all of these as long as you are prepared to be flexible about the way you study. Although you have developed a study style that answers the needs of secondary schooling, you will need to adapt it to fit the new demands at university.

Remember that you're a professional student, an adult who is studying (if only you were making lots of money doing it!) as a full-time occupation. Some of you will study part-time, but even so you need to approach it professionally.

At university, you are responsible for your own study. The teachers will not be there to check on your progress. However, one advantage of being responsible for your own learning is that you are free to consider your personal preferences.

Different people like to study in different ways

For example, different students may

- like to try something 'hands on' before they fully understand it
- be very good at visualising the process or issues
- prefer to talk something through with a friend to help both of them understand it
- like to study late at night, or early in the morning
- use their computers for everything from notes to drafts to study timetables.

While it's important to take these preferences into consideration, you must also realise that studying law at university is different from the study you have done at secondary school, and that you'll need to adapt.

TAKE SOME TIME TO EXPLORE YOUR STUDY SELF

There are many ways you can find out more about your personal learning style. We've included a brief questionnaire at the end of this book (Appendix II). There are also resources available via the Web: you can do online tests and get a brief evaluation of yourself. Two good places to start are the page of IQ and Personality tests <http://www.2h.com/tests/personality.phtm> or you can try Yahoo! for some links <http://www.yahoo.com/Science/Psychology/>

Once you have thought about your preferences, it's time to put them to work. Knowing a lot about your personal style is only helpful if you are also adapting and using good study techniques. Work from your strengths and be prepared to compensate for your weaknesses.

Most of the assessment tasks you will face as a law student will require you to have a good mental grasp of the material under discussion. It won't be enough to memorise facts; you need to understand ideas.

> Just as our eyes need light in order to see, our minds need ideas in order to conceive.
>
> Nicholas Malebranche, 1675

Engaging actively with the work you have to do involves questioning and evaluating your tasks. Sometimes you'll have to make decisions about what's important, what you need to do more work on, and what you don't.

ESSENTIAL STUDY SKILLS

How well do you need to understand the concepts you are being introduced to? There are (at least) four levels of understanding.

Level 1: *'I remember seeing that before'*

This is the basic level of understanding: recognising something that you have experienced before. This is not particularly useful at tertiary level. You may think that you can approach open book exams with only this level of knowledge—'I'll know the right answer when I see it'—but it won't necessarily work (see Chapter 10 on exams).

Level 2: *'I understand the beginning and the middle, but I can't see why the judgment follows'*

At the next level of understanding, you can remember bits of the whole concept, but you need prompting to complete it. This is a good stage to get to, because you can easily build on it. Doing some extra reading or talking the issue over with friends should help deepen your understanding.

Level 3: *'Let me explain this to you'*

After that, you can develop a knowledge of something that enables you to remember the whole of the issue. This means that you can explain it to someone else. You already have this level of knowledge for a great many things—the rules of your favourite sport, the plot of your favourite soapie, the legendary figures important in the history of your hobby.

If you develop this level of knowledge in law, you'll do very well in assessments.

Level 4: *'I think that this concept applies in this case, too'*

The highest level of knowing occurs when you have not only made the accepted principles part of your own knowledge base, but when you can adapt them to new situations, or even develop them further through mentally manipulating them.

BECOMING AN ACTIVE LEARNER

In order to reach the higher levels of knowing, you need to become active with the material. Study techniques such as reading and re-reading the same information in the very same words, or writing out your notes over and over, are passive techniques. At university level, you won't have time to study this way.

Active learning is more valuable

First, it allows you to interact with the concepts you need to learn, even if it's only mentally, and that means that study is much more interesting.

Second, active learning is more time efficient. Certainly, some of the things you do may take longer than just reading over your notes. However, they are also more effective. You will learn more in the same time, or the same amount in a shorter time, which will be very handy for those of you with combined courses and very full timetables.

Third, active learning encourages you to think creatively about the material. You will discover that at university level, there is not always one right answer that you need to know; your task will increasingly be to analyse and evaluate

ESSENTIAL STUDY SKILLS

different applications in specific instances. Active learning will help to stimulate your ability to do this because it encourages analytical and creative thinking.

Here is a list of some suggested active learning strategies:

- Make a flow-chart of the facts of a case instead of listing them—this will help you to remember how each of the parties is related and what their duties and obligations are. Flow charts are good for visualising torts cases where the issue is one of causation. A spatial diagram provides useful exercise for the brain and can help you gain a critical perspective.
- Draw a diagram of the events of a case instead of reading them over again—you will always need to use your imagination to picture the circumstances of a particular case. If you have read the facts several times you may find a diagram a useful way of both resting and re-stimulating your mind. Diagrams are particularly useful in motor vehicle accident cases.
- Organise a debate with your friends where you can take sides representing the different actors in the case—it is always helpful to find out what other students are thinking. You may in fact reassess your approach towards a topic once you have discussed the ideas with others. If you intend to go to the Bar, you need all of this sort of practice you can get.
- Turn dense paragraphs into point-form lists—particularly useful for later use as stimuli for turning the points into coherent paragraphs, such as those you need in essay exams.
- Rewrite complex material into everyday language; practise explaining concepts to 'the person in the street'—this may give you a new perspective on the 'reasonable person' idea. It's quite a challenge to explain complex notions from your specialised area to someone whose mind follows completely different convolutions.
- Formulate your own questions on sections of material

you need to learn; try to imagine you are setting the exam—this helps you identify the important issues.
- Summarise complicated cases or concepts into a newspaper-style article—or you may like to try working out what the 'real' facts of a case might be from the short media versions you see everyday. There are versions and versions, and all of them have truth at some level.
- Do a 10-minute analytical brainstorm—spend the first five minutes listing all the advantageous aspects of one legal theory, and then the next five minutes enumerating the positives of an alternative theory.

Of course, there will be basic principles that you need to know before you can test various approaches against them. However, you need to remember that in law, what is 'true' or 'right' is always in the process of development.

IDEAS FOR COLLABORATIVE LEARNING

This leads us to collaborative learning. Many of your fellow students will be struggling under the same demanding workload as you are. It may be that, by pooling your resources, you can be of mutual benefit to each other. Talking over concepts and attempting to put forward your own point of view in a friendly group can be very helpful to your own—and everyone else's—understanding of the concepts.

Some collaborative learning tasks that you can share with others are simple, such as sharing out photocopying duties. Others are a bit more of a challenge—and therefore more interesting and rewarding—such as setting up mock debates in which you can argue about issues or judgments. Another way to collaborate could be to role play characters in the cases in order to get a good grasp of what the different issues were for everyone concerned. The crux of collab-

ESSENTIAL STUDY SKILLS

orative learning is to share and enhance everyone's learning and understanding, not to copy others' ideas.

TAKING ADVANTAGE OF THE WAY MEMORY WORKS

'Interesting things are easy to remember'

We know that repeating things over and over is one way to remember them, but there are other factors that help us to make and retain permanent memories. For example, if you are really interested in something, you have no trouble remembering all the details about it. Most people have no difficulty remembering the plot intricacies of a favourite book, film or TV show. You can probably remember the detailed and complex rules of your favourite hobby, sport or computer game. Because you are *motivated* to know these things, they are easy to recall.

This means that you need to be motivated, for example, to find out why the judgment was made as it was, and also to be very interested in how this may affect later decisions.

Another element of memory is *understanding*. If you know how something works, you can easily recall the details without learning them off by heart, because you can relate the different sections to one another. So understanding a concept will help you to remember it. When you first learned the 12 times table it was a collection of numbers. When you began to understand the concept, the numbers made sense because you understood how they related to each other. That is, you need to develop a context and structure so that you can then see how the details fit in.

Along the same line, if you can appreciate the *organisation* of a certain system, then you can more easily recall the separate parts that contribute to that system. We find it easier to remember items that we can fit neatly into categories, because we like to see (or imagine) patterns in the data. Therefore being able to organise the information coherently will aid memory. When you made connections and saw the patterns in the times tables (12 x 5 is the same as 5 x 12), they were much easier to remember.

Similarly, *linking* items together will help you to remember them. If you can't see an overall pattern, perhaps you can see a similarity to a case you already know. Associating one idea with another known idea will aid recall.

Finally, if we consider the sensory material that we are receiving, we realise that most of what we learn reaches us through sight. Having the ability to *visualise* something enhances memory, and being able to visualise something as a three-dimensional image is an even stronger enhancement. If the facts of the case can become a story in your head, so that you can imagine the people involved (or even give them names—see Chapter 6, 'Reading case law'), you will remember the details easily.

The study suggestions in the last two chapters are meant to help you get motivated and organised. If you can manage to get these under control, then you will be well on the way to success in your law studies.

Part II
UNDERSTANDING LAW

5 CRUCIAL CONCEPTS

'When *I* use a word,' Humpty Dumpty said in a rather scornful tone, 'it means just what I choose it to mean— neither more nor less.'
   Lewis Carroll, *Through the Looking Glass* (1872)

A big part of removing the mystique of law is understanding its crucial concepts. If you can get hold of these ideas early, you will save yourself much time, trouble and heartache later in the year.

Law often appears in technical language, the meaning of which is not always apparent to the uninitiated. It may be written in Latin (*ultra vires, mens rea*), French (*chose in action, en ventre sa mère*) or in obscure English ('devise' = give land by will, 'determine' = bring to an end). A good legal dictionary is therefore an important reference tool (see Appendix I for some recommended reading).

In this chapter, we focus on some of the crucial concepts that are often presumed in law. We begin with the different meanings of the word 'law', and then move on to some of the other concepts that will help you get started.

STUDYING LAW AT UNIVERSITY

'LAW'—A ROSE BY ANY OTHER NAME STILL HAS THORNS

In this chapter, we look at some of the most basic concepts of law and give you some good working definitions. Some common terms are listed in the box below.

> **Basic terms in law**
>
> *law* A 'body of enacted or customary rules recognised by a community as binding' (OED). The precise significance of such 'rules' and the way in which they are 'recognised' remains the subject of much dispute. Different definitions of what law is are often best understood as coming from distinct theoretical positions on what law does. There is a basic conflict, for example, between:
>
> (a) positive law: Positivists argue that law properly understood is restricted to rules laid down in advance by those who have ultimate power in a political community. An influential positivist is John Austin, who defined law as the command of the Sovereign backed up by sanctions.
>
> (b) natural law (or moral law): Natural law theorists believe that above and beyond any positive law is the law of nature, an expression of some supreme universal force (often Divine) that provides a system of justice common to all human beings.
>
> **Cross-check:** *See further the discussion of legal theory in Chapter 6.*
>
> *common law* This originally meant the unwritten law that was said to be 'common' to the whole of England. It

CRUCIAL CONCEPTS

now refers to the body of legal principles that have been developed by the decisions of English courts. The way in which this body of law develops is discussed in Chapter 5: 'Reading case law'. Commonwealth countries received the common law from England but exist as independent jurisdictions. Australia became a fully independent jurisdiction when appeals to English courts were abolished in 1986. By contrast, the English Privy Council remains the final court of appeal for cases arising in New Zealand.

The term 'common law' may be used in a number of distinct ways. It is often used in opposition to:

(a) statute law: Laws created by Acts of Parliament rather than the courts.

(b) equity law: The body of rules formerly administered by the Court of Chancery. These were originally intended to temper the strict, rule-based common law with natural justice and fairness. Over time, however, it also developed into a body of rules.

(c) civil law: In this context, referring to Roman law. This now encompasses the legal systems of most of continental Europe and is characterised by the codification of large areas of law and relative freedom from the constraints of precedent. (See also civil law/criminal law.)

precedent The doctrine of *stare decisis* [to stand by things decided] that governs the development of the common law. See Chapter 6: 'Reading case Law'.

civil law/criminal law In this context, civil law refers to law pertaining to matters between private individuals (similar to private law, but see also common law), and criminal law refers to the law and proceedings dealing with punishment by the State. It is important to note that a single event may have both civil and criminal consequences. For example, if A unlawfully injures B, B may

> bring a civil action against A in tort, seeking a remedy (usually damages (money)). This requires B to prove her case on the balance of probabilities. The State may bring criminal proceedings against A for his criminal wrong, and impose a fine or gaol term. This requires the State to prove its case beyond reasonable doubt.
>
> *public law/private law* Public law concerns transactions involving the State, whereas private law deals with legal relationships between private individuals. The former thus includes constitutional and administrative law, while the latter includes torts, contracts, property and the like. Criminal law is sometimes treated as part of public law, sometimes as a category of its own. Note that civil law jurisdictions (such as continental Europe) make more of this distinction, sometimes to the point of having a separate law of contract when the State is a party.

A few more useful concepts are given below.

> **Further useful terms and definitions**
>
> *cause of action* The circumstance(s) giving rise to a right to bring a legal action.
>
> *tort* A breach of duty. The duty may arise from a personal relation (e.g. negligence and the duty of care) or from a contract. It is a civil injury that gives rise to a cause of action on the part of the injured party. A tortfeasor is a person who commits a tort.
>
> *remedy* The means by which a wrong is redressed or prevented.
>
> *indictable/summary offence* In criminal law, an indictable offence is a more serious offence and is triable by jury. A summary offence may be tried before a magistrate

CONCEPTS

> only. This has been altered by statute in some jurisdictions.
>
> *corporation* An artificial legal entity. The corporation is a separate legal person from its shareholders (contributors of capital) and officers (managers). Two reasons for its importance as a legal structure are:
>
> (a) perpetual succession: Property held by the corporation is not affected by changes in its human shareholders and officers.
>
> (b) limited liability: In a limited ('Ltd') company (a type of corporation), the liability of the company's human shareholders is limited to any money owing on their shares. In legislation, 'person' will usually include corporations. Where corporations are to be excluded, 'natural person' may be used.
>
> *barrister/solicitor* A barrister's main function is to act as an advocate in court. A solicitor is involved in the administration and processing of legal business more generally. This may include the giving of legal advice, preparing cases for litigation and representing clients in court. In some jurisdictions, only barristers can appear in certain courts.

LANGUAGE IS POWER

> Lexicographer: A writer of dictionaries, a harmless drudge.
>
> Dr Johnson, *A Dictionary of the English Language* (1755)

See Appendix I for further reading.

6 READING CASE LAW

> But though I do not understand the ground upon which the case proceeded, it is a case which has stood for fifty years, and ... I am satisfied that it is now too late to interfere with the decision.
> *Wheeler v New Merton Board Mills* [1933] 2 KB 669, 691 (Scrutton LJ).

[In other words, old cases never die—they just lose their appeal ...]

A common problem faced by law students, and other students who read case law for their studies, is that they might spend an hour reading a judgment from start to end and gain nothing from it.

In this chapter, we explain some ways to make reading law reports easier, and to improve your retention of what you read.

head in the case

READING CASE LAW

BEFORE YOU TURN A PAGE...

'Why are you reading?'

Here we are, back to that question again. Case law (or judge-made law) is the basis of common law and, along with statute law, is an important source of law in a common law legal system. Many areas of the law, such as negligence, have developed without a legislative basis. That is, the areas were not legislated specifically; the laws dealing with that area have grown up around a number of cases that have been considered in that area. In order to understand 'the law', then, it is necessary to understand the cases that make it up and their significance. Consider the cases you are referred to: what is the context for each? Think about the area of law of which the case is a component. Why is this case important? Why is it on the reading list? It may help to use the following categories to divide up cases.

Foundation cases

These are cases that make a major change to the law or establish a new doctrine. This happens when a superior court (such as the High Court, or the House of Lords) makes a decision that overrules previous authority; for example, the 'neighbour' principle in *Donoghue v Stevenson* in the cases referred to below.

> *Donoghue v Stevenson* [1932] AC 562. This case established the 'neighbour' principle on which the modern action in negligence is founded. As may be seen by reading the cases that lead up to *Donoghue v Stevenson*, however, this was not merely a decision 'out of the blue', but was the culmination of a series of cases that had extended the idea of responsibility for one's actions outside of contractual relationships.

> *Jaensch v Coffey* (1984) 155 CLR 549. Here, Deane J introduced the notion of proximity to operate as a limit on the 'neighbour' principle developed in *Donoghue v Stevenson*.
>
> *Lynch v Lynch* (1991) 25 NSWLR 411. Note the policy questions raised here: see, e.g. Fiona Forsyth's 'Case Note' (1992) 18 *Melbourne University Law Review* 950.
>
> *Cook v Cook* (1986) 162 CLR 376

Frontier cases

Because such 'foundational' decisions are dependent on the circumstances of the case, they cannot always set out general guidelines that will cover future scenarios adequately. Subsequent cases must therefore map out in an incremental way the detail of the new doctrine. Consider, for example, Deane J's 'three stage test' for duty in *Jaensch v Coffey* (the reference is shown above).

Example cases

Example cases apply doctrine to new fact situations. They are important as an example of how to approach new scenarios. An example is the extension of duty of care to include a mother's duty to her unborn child (to drive carefully) in *Lynch v Lynch*, as above.

Supporting cases

Some cases may be used by a court as an opportunity to reaffirm a doctrine. These cases give added authority to the doctrine; for example, the majority support for Deane J's proximity test in *Cook v Cook*, given above. Note that these categories may overlap. For instance, *Jaensch v Coffey* could also be considered an example case applying duty to a plaintiff who claims to have suffered 'nervous shock', and *Cook v Cook* stands for more than merely supporting Deane J's proximity test. With all this in mind, we are ready to look at the case in question.

OK, NOW TURN A FEW PAGES...

'Judgments ain't Agatha Christie'

You should not approach case law the way you would a literary text. Judgments are not written for artistic purposes: they are written to justify a decision relating to the particular circumstances of the case and, often, to make more general points on a disputed area of law. They are there to be picked apart and have relevant principles distilled from them. Your approach should reflect this. That's why it's important to keep asking questions as you read: be analytical about the relevance and significance of what you are reading.

It is very, very hard to read a long case from start to end and make sense of the whole thing. Instead, it may be useful to try the following approach. This is similar to the general guidelines on skim reading which we talked about previously (see Chapter 3), but here we apply it specifically to case law. Although it may seem a little like you are jumping around the text, using this approach is usually more helpful than plunging straight into a 200-page judgment.

What are you looking for?

As we have explained above, you read judgments for four basic reasons:

- to understand better the area of the law under consideration
- to find out what the case adds to the law
- to know the relative importance of the case, and
- to become familiar with the processes of judicial reasoning.

If you are expected to read only one aspect of a judgment (e.g. the brief discussion of negligence in a voluminous case on estoppel), it is often unnecessary to go far beyond the sections of the judgment discussing the relevant point. Do not expect to understand fully the discussion of an area of law with which you are unfamiliar—always keep in mind what you are looking for.

Read the headnote

The headnote is the summary at the top of the case written by the editors of the law report. It does not form part of the case and is not binding. You cannot cite a headnote (see Chapter 8 for a discussion of citation in law essays). The headnote may, however, provide a summary of the facts and a breakdown of the court's reasoning.

If there is more than one judge, note the judges who make up the majority (if there is one). As their judgments will contain the case's *ratio decidendi* (see below), you should probably read them first. Note that judgments are usually printed in order of the judge's seniority rather than in any logical sequence to do with the case.

Get the story straight

Law is difficult to understand and is of little use in isolation from people and events. If the headnote does not give you a clear picture of what has happened, skim through the judgments for an outline of the 'material facts'. These are not merely important to understanding the decision, but to showing that its significance may be restricted to particular circumstances.

If the case is an appeal case (and most cases you will study are), be especially careful to work out who the parties are. The appellant in an appeal case, for example, may have been the defendant in the original case. Therefore it will usually be easier to think of the facts in terms of plaintiff (person who has suffered damage) and defendant (person allegedly responsible for the damage) rather than 'appellant' and 'respondent'.

Kerrigan's case in *The Castle*

You may like to draw the relationships out schematically, as shown in Figure 6.1 on the following page.

Know the legal history

Judgments in an appeal are in response to previous findings by another court or courts. If the headnote does not inform you of the history, skim the opening of each judgment to find out who won in the previous trial and why. For example, a judgment may begin 'This is an appeal against a decision of the...' At other times, you may have to do a bit of detective work—good places to look are at the end of the headnote and the end of the judgments.

Cheat—find out how it ends

You should never, ever, be surprised by the eventual outcome of a case. If you are, it indicates that either the judgment has been written by Hercule Poirot (gathering

STUDYING LAW AT UNIVERSITY

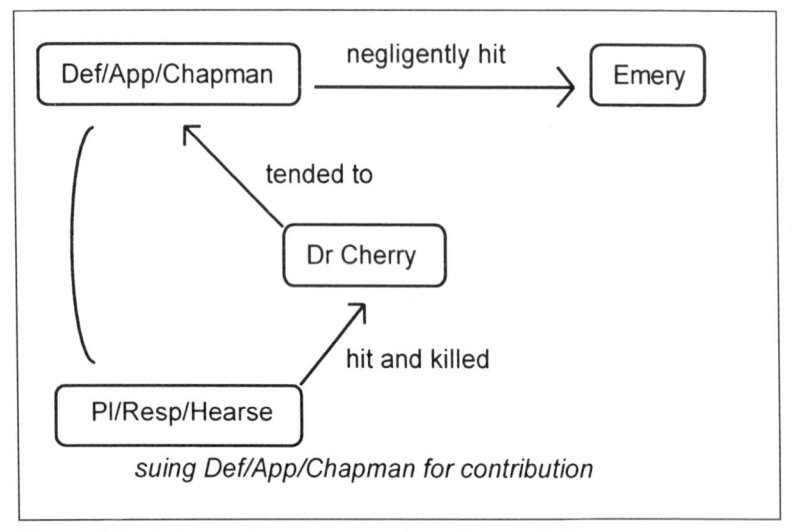

Figure 6.1: Schematic representation of a case's facts

(Def/App/Chapman negligently hit Emery; Def/App/Chapman tended to Dr Cherry; Pl/Resp/Hearse hit and killed Dr Cherry; Pl/Resp/Hearse suing Def/App/Chapman for contribution)

together the suspects after dinner and then revealing that the butler did it), or you have not been paying attention while you read. To avoid this, always look at the headnote to find out the end of each judgment, and from the orders at the end of each judgment and finally the order at the end of the last judgment, what the result is. Then make sure you know who the dissenting judges are (if any).

Now you are ready to start reading.

> *Ratio decidendi* and *Obiter dicta*
>
> What is the ratio?
> The *ratio decidendi* of a case is the argument or reasoning on which the ultimate decision is based. Note that each judge may have his or her own ratio, but that the ratio of a case is the reasoning of the majority of the judges.

READING CASE LAW

> Why is the ratio important?
> Any statement of the law logically necessary to this reasoning is binding on a lower court. For example, if the Australian High Court holds that it can't (or won't) fix a standard of care in circumstances where to do so would sanction a breach of the law (Gala v Preston (1991) 172 CLR 243), no Australian court of law other than the High Court itself can contradict that ruling. Note, however, that it may be possible to distinguish the case (i.e. to say that because of the specific circumstances, the rule does not apply). Note also, for example, that decisions of the Supreme Courts of other states are not binding on Victorian courts but are usually 'highly persuasive'.
>
> *Obiter dicta* refers to statements on a point of law which are not part of the ratio and are therefore not binding on a lower court. Examples of *obiter dicta* are typically:
>
> - discussion of legal doctrine not applicable in the circumstances, and
> - discussion of relevant doctrine as it might apply to hypothetical circumstances.

SKIM, READ, NOTE AND REVIEW

'Judgments ain't poetry'

> Almost certainly, the respondent gave no thought to these matters. It is probably only bored lawyers or travel executives who, in the solitude of a ship or airline cabin, actually read the fine print of terms and conditions such as those relied upon by the appellant here.
> *Baltic Shipping Co v Dillon* (1991)
> 22 NSWLR 1, 25 (Kirby P)

Almost there! Now that you know what the judgment is basically about, it's time to start reading for a little detail.

Skim (again)
Even at this point it is worth skimming the judgments so that you know what parts of each judgment are important for your purposes, and the stages an individual judge reaches on the way to his/her final decision.

Read—and think at the same time
When you read, you should be thinking not merely 'What does this paragraph mean?' but much more specifically 'How does this paragraph fit into the conclusion that this judge makes? How does this paragraph compare to my understanding of this area of law?'

Take notes
No one expects students to memorise cases, but you should be familiar with them. Your notes should enable you to recall the facts and important legal principles of each case, but there is no point compiling reams of five-page case summaries. This would take months and be ultimately useless for your understanding, or in an exam.

Examples of what you might usefully include in your notes are shown in Figure 6.2 opposite.

Review—and do it soon
After reading all relevant parts of the judgment, it is worth skimming back over the text and perhaps also over the headnote to see if it accurately reflects the content. Make some more notes about your impression of the legal importance of the case. Compare this to a textbook. Then open up another volume of the CLRs ...

READING CASE LAW

Name of case	*Chapman v Hearse*
Year and court	1961, HC
Brief statement of the facts	Def/App/Chapman negligently hit E Dr Cherry tending to Def on road negligently hit and killed by Pl/Resp/Hearse
Legal history	Cherry dependants won action (Wrongs Act) v Hearse, who sued Chapman (Wrongs Act) for contribution.
	Hearse won at lower courts, Chapman appealing
Judicial reasoning	Duty
	The injury to a class of persons including 'Good Samaritans' is 'reasonably foreseeable' as consequence of collision
	Policy is to encourage rescuers/heroes
	Not necessary to foresee the exact sequence of events leading to harm
	Causation
	Whether an intervening act severs the causal connection is 'a matter of circumstance and degree'
	Cannot exclude acts from what is reasonably foreseeable solely on the ground that they were wrongful
Result and order	For the PL/RESP/HEARSE
	Chapman must pay 1/4 of Hearse's damages owing to Cherry dependants

Figure 6.2: Sample notes: who, what, where, how, why

INTRODUCING LEGAL THEORY

> No theory is good except on condition that one uses it to go beyond.
>
> André Gide

One of the most important aspects of studying legal theory or jurisprudence is coming to terms with 'theory'. In this chapter, we look at what theory is and the ways in which theoretical perspectives are used to better understand the law.

WHAT IS THEORY?

Ways of thinking about law

When you look at the way the law functions, it is easy to become bogged down with the rules that must be applied and the facts to which they relate. This can prevent you gaining a broader understanding of the forces that determine those rules and shape their application to particular circumstances.

The use of theory helps us to analyse the value and belief systems that support our understanding of what law is for, and the basis of our belief in it.

In short, we use theories of law to move from thinking about what the law is in a certain situation, to considering why the law is what it is.

INTRODUCING LEGAL THEORY

HOW MUCH DO I HAVE TO KNOW?

Introducing the perspectives

It is important to understand that for as long as people have been governed by law, people have been arguing about the theories behind it. In most legal theory or jurisprudence courses you will not be expected to understand fully all of the complex debates that have occupied legal theorists. The aim is rather to:

- introduce you to some of the ongoing debates that are important in the study of law, and
- enable you to engage critically with some of the different perspectives that inform these debates, and with your own values and viewpoints.

Rather than spending your time looking for the 'right' answer, you need to think about understanding how the different perspectives are argued—what point(s) of law or what theory they are based on.

SOME LEVELS OF ANALYSIS

Breaking down theory

It often helps to consider what a particular theory is trying to do. Different theories aim at understanding different aspects of the law. That is, the theories are attempts to explain what the law means, what it is and what it is (or should be) doing in our society. In this section, we divide legal theories into three basic categories:

- Theories that consider the concrete workings of the law—does our abstract notion of justice accord with the reality of the way the law operates?
- Theories that seek to understand the function of law in our society—what is the basis of this notion of justice?
- Theories that challenge the idea of law itself—on what basis do we assume the objectivity and impartiality of the law (or any knowledge system)? Is the law trying to achieve 'justice', or does it perhaps have some other aim?

Note that these categories are merely used to provide a basic framework and are not comprehensive or even fixed.

The concrete workings of the law

For most people, 'justice' at least includes a requirement that the law should treat people equally. However, empirical studies (i.e. studies based on observation of what is happening in the real world using, for example, statistical studies) are often used to demonstrate that claims of equality before the law are not matched in reality. This is not so much a theoretical perspective as a challenge to the theory behind law.

For example, studies of Aboriginal peoples under white rule in Australia have revealed that their physical treatment, the social and economic effects of dispossession, and the broader effects of political disempowerment have led to a situation where Aboriginal Australians are far more likely to go to gaol than non-Aboriginal Australians. This raises questions about our belief that 'everyone is equal before the law'.

Similarly, studies of the position of women in society—the way in which property rights were refused to women, the ways in which women are stereotyped by the law—challenge the assumption that men and women are equal before the law.

It is argued by some theorists that other studies of the

significance of race and ethnicity, of intellectual and physical disability, and of sexuality, show that the law does not treat all people equally. Therefore, since the practice of law does not appear to correspond to the theoretical equality behind it, we may begin to question the applicability of that theoretical framework.

At this level of analysis, however, the question of law reform is very much within the existing legal framework. That is, we are asking can the law be improved to make it operate more equally?

Changes to legislation, decisions by the courts, and the use of regulations, all ultimately accept the structures that support and give legitimacy to the law and what justice is seen to be. In the second level of analysis, we look at how we come to understand this notion of 'justice', while in the third level we look more deeply at the presumption that law can ever be objective and impartial.

The function of law in society

What, then, is the theoretical framework of the law?

Here we are really considering what purpose law serves in society. This in turn leads us to consider the relationship between individual people and society as a whole. Most legal theories fit into one of two groups, depending on whether they view this relationship between the one and the many as essentially consensual or conflictual.

- Do people basically get along with one another? Is the role of law merely to keep the peace, to smooth over problems? (The Consensual Model of Society.)
- Or, is society a restraint on individuals, keeping them from descending into anarchy? Is the role of law to prevent such conflict? (The Conflictual Model of Society.)

When we come to think about the relationship between individuals and society, the dominant philosophy is liberalism.

> **Liberalism and its alternatives**
>
> Classical liberalism holds that individuals are rational, free and equal. Everyone benefits from a society where everyone is free to exercise his or her rights so long as they do not infringe the rights of others. The role of the law should be minimal, directed to enforcing bargains and protecting individuals from the state.
>
> You can contrast this understanding of society with alternative social orders. For example, there has long been a debate within Chinese society over the proper ordering of society. On the one hand, *li* (or Confucianism) refers to a society based on rules of moral conduct, where everyone knows their place in the social hierarchy ('the rule of man'). On the other, *fa* (or Legalism) refers to a society based on legal rules so as to maintain social order ('the rule of law').
>
> You can also contrast liberalism with the possibility of a plurality of legal systems, such as the inclusion of Aboriginal customary law.

It is useful to think about questions such as what role law plays in each of these conceptions of society. Is the law reactive (maintaining order, preventing change), or progressive (bringing about change, redressing imbalances)?

> **Thinking about the alternatives**
>
> Various methodologies have been developed that may help you consider the function that law plays in society:
>
> - Comparative law—What can you learn from comparing our legal system to other legal

> systems? Is there a danger in thinking that we can simply look at the ways in which different legal structures work without considering broader cultural and historical factors?
> - Functionalism—Does law merely fulfil a role in society? How might we think about the legal system if we look at society as a type of machine made up of many subsystems (including law, the family, government and the economy) each with a specific function? Is this helpful?
> - Law and Economics—The law and economics approach sees the role of law as reflecting principles of supply and demand aimed at 'wealth maximisation'. Does this help improve our understanding of the legal system?

Critiquing the law itself—undermining the objectivity of law

This level of analysis considers fundamental perspectives. When we speak about the 'objectivity' of law, and its claims to 'universality', essentially we are attempting to move beyond looking at the way in which the law works, and the function that the law serves, to consider how it is that we have come to think of law as 'law'. On what basis do we acknowledge certain 'rights'? Are they simply self-evident, or do they have their own function? How do we come to decide what is 'just'? Are the purported ideals of law ever achievable, or is law really fulfilling some other agenda?

Here, again, we will break this down. First we will look at critiques that take substantive problems as their basis for critique. Then we will turn to more theoretically based critiques that challenge claims of objectivity more generally.

Critiquing law at a substantive level

The fact that law does not treat everyone equally may not only reveal flaws in its claims to universal justice, but may in fact reveal values and prejudices within the idea of law itself.

Marxism thus claims that law may serve as a tool by which to perpetuate class inequalities. The fact that the law protects property rights prevents a more equitable allocation of resources. This, according to Marxism, occurs in order to enable the rich to maintain power over the poor (the landless, the proletariat). Law is thus an instrument of the ruling classes and true equality must be sought through revolution. (Note, however, E. P. Thompson's view that the rule of law nevertheless acts to restrain the excesses of the ruling class.)

Similarly, various schools of feminism argue that law functions as a means of reinforcing male authority (patriarchy). The law for many years did not recognise women as persons (they had to bring actions in court through their husbands). Today, the formal equality of men and women arguably masks women's disempowerment (in property disputes in family law, the 'reasonable man/person' in negligence, etc.). In the same way, the 'public/private dichotomy' refers to the law's hesitancy about getting involved in disputes seen to be 'domestic'. This clearly has greater implications for women than for men.

Schools of feminism

It is important to distinguish between various schools of feminism. The 'schools' are not necessarily separate entities, but reflect different approaches to the question of women's equality. In their own way, theories of feminism attempt to explain the relationship between women and society at large, or women's place within society. The main differences between the theories concern the political framework within which people operate, and the question of how women differ from men.

- Difference, or standpoint feminism: This school maintains that women hold a different perspective from men. One version of this is Carol Gilligan's 'different voice' thesis.
- Radical feminism: According to radical feminism, women's disempowerment is a structural fact of patriarchy and is intricately bound up in heterosexual relationships.
- Liberal feminism: Liberal feminists believe that women can 'work within the system' to bring about change.
- Poststructuralist (or postmodern) feminism: Postmodern feminists propose that women's disempowerment is tied to the construction of 'female'. They believe that change must be sought through looking at the power relations that define such social roles.

Critiquing law at a theoretical level

At a more theoretical level, other approaches look more generally at the claims of law to objectivity. The belief that knowledge can be objective (that is, true for all people at all times in all places) and that we can apply such a scientific perspective to social questions is an important part of the belief that the law can be fair for all people.

Critical Legal Studies (or 'CLS') directly challenges law's claims to objectivity, and is linked with Marxist critiques of its substantive provisions.

Poststructuralism and postmodernism refer to broader theoretical approaches that are critical of claims to objectivity in general. These approaches challenge the authority (and author-ity) of legal discourse. What are the implications if the 'individual' subject of law is in fact not unitary but fractured? What does it mean if the meanings in the texts of law are not fixed but represent a power game that establishes itself as the medium and the content of truth? Such challenges transform law into a site of contestation.

APPLYING THE THEORIES

> A theorist without practice is a tree without fruit; and a devotee without learning is a house without an entrance.
> Sa'Di, 1258 (translated by James Ross)

Where do you stand?

Where, in all of this, do you stand? The most effective way to learn more about these theories is to apply them yourself. Which level of analysis do you think is the most helpful in understanding 'the law'? Which approach do you think best reflects the way in which the law operates?

It is important to remember that you do not have to confine yourself to one perspective. In fact, it is probable that you will find different parts of many theoretical approaches are helpful in different areas of law.

Some areas you may want to consider in particular are:

- Theories of judicial decision-making—How do judges reach their decisions?
- Questions of law reform—How and why do we change the law?
- Legal education—How is the law taught? What perspectives are emphasised?

INTRODUCING LEGAL THEORY

MORE STUDY HINTS

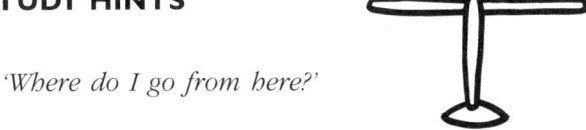

'Where do I go from here?'

Finally, here are three pieces of advice for studying legal theory—whether as a single course or as a component of a larger course:

1. THINK in terms of themes

The only way to understand these theories better is to engage with them. This means not only reading the texts, but while you are reading, thinking about them and looking for points in common. You can start by thinking about each theory and each text in terms of the themes discussed in this chapter. Ask yourself these questions:

- At what level is the author (and/or perhaps the judge) approaching the question?
- What approach is she or he advocating?

Take notes while you read, but remember that although summaries of articles may be useful, it is better to have a broad understanding of each area of the course. If you are studying for an exam, you should prepare brief notes with issues raised under each heading of the course. Use your reading guide to make sure you have covered everything you need to.

Cross-check: *See Chapter 9 on exam preparation.*

2. TALK about the themes

Get involved in class discussion (especially if you have done the reading). Don't worry too much about saying the wrong thing or sounding foolish—these theoretical perspectives will be new to everyone, and the best way to learn how to apply them is through talking about them. If you are uncertain about how the theory relates to the subject matter, ask.

Informal study groups may help you to apply the theories. Try collaborative learning: get half a dozen students together, perhaps each preparing an area of the course. The aim should not be merely to exchange notes, however, but to stimulate conversation.

Cross-check: *See Chapter 4 for more ideas on effective study.*

3. RELAX

Most legal theory examinations and many essays are intended to be reflective. This means that you are not required to demonstrate a complete understanding of all the legal philosophy touched on in the course, but that you need to show that you have:

- done (most of) the reading
- thought about the course, and
- gained a basic understanding of the historical and philosophical underpinnings of the legal system, and some of the critiques of those underpinnings.

Cross-check: *There is more about relaxing and controlling panic in Chapter 10.*

Part III
USING THE LAW

8 WRITING LAW ESSAYS

> Circumstantial evidence is a very tricky thing. It may seem to point very straight to one thing, but if you shift your own point of view a little, you may find it pointing in an equally uncompromising manner to something entirely different.
>
> Sherlock Holmes in *The Boscombe Valley Mystery*,
> Sir Arthur Conan Doyle

Legal writing may present particular difficulties to students unaccustomed to the subject matter and style. This chapter discusses how best to use your research time, and how to present your work.

Basic essay writing skills such as structure, organisation, and editing are briefly discussed here (you will find some further references in Appendix I, from your institution's study skills unit, and in your departmental guide). Similarly, this chapter does not discuss particular legal research methods. Your law librarians will be able to assist you in this regard.

ESSAY WRITING: THE BASICS

Writing essays at university is a more demanding task than, for example, writing essays at high school. Here we will mention the essential concepts; you will find more detailed information on essay writing elsewhere (see Appendix I).

First, a tertiary level essay must have structure. In general this means a recognisable beginning (introduction), middle (main body) and end (conclusion). There should be clear links between these sections, with the conclusion matching what was proposed in the introduction (no place for surprise endings here). It's good to have a plan in mind (or on paper) as you start reading for your essay, because you can identify where pieces of information will be useful in the final essay. Plans can change as you find out more about the topic, but at least you have the beginnings of a structure.

Second, a good essay is well organised, as a good case should be. The pieces of information you have gathered from your reading should be presented logically, along with your interpretations of both the topic and the readings, and the relevance of the readings to the proposition under discussion. Remember that you must clearly distinguish between the opinions of authors you have consulted and your own work.

Third, it's important that you give yourself time to edit your essay. At university level, the first draft will probably not meet all the marking criteria. Try to write at least two drafts (this is a little easier now with current wordprocessing software, and most institutions will not accept assignments that have not been wordprocessed). You will need to edit your work for a number of factors: for the ideas and whether they hold together; for the clarity of the argument you are proposing; for the referencing conventions (more about this below); for simple factors such as spelling, punctuation, and grammar; and for presentation. This means that you should proofread your essay a few times before you hand it in: once for argument, once for referencing, and so on.

One more thought: try not to edit as you write. It's very hard to be a creator and a critic at the same time. It is more practical to write as much as you can, and then edit out the less good parts later.

RESEARCH FOR YOUR ESSAY

> Men occasionally stumble over the truth, but most pick themselves up and hurry off as if nothing had happened.
> Winston Churchill

'Don't miss the forest for the trees'

Perhaps the greatest problem that many students encounter when preparing to write an essay in law is detail. It is easy to find yourself wading through complex 200-page judgments or heady articles by learned academics, slowly losing sight of what it all means in terms of the end product.

This is a case of not seeing the forest for the trees. (An analogy particularly relevant for students who waste reams of paper making photocopies that they never read!)

When you are preparing for an essay, it is as important to structure your approach to the subject matter as it is to structure the words you write. If you are unfamiliar with an area of law, opening the latest High Court judgment on the topic may be of little assistance. You must remember judges do not necessarily write to simplify areas of law; their main objective is to justify a particular decision. Similarly, a journal article may not provide the best introduction to a topic, because the author is presenting her or his particular view on the topic rather than explaining the topic itself. Instead, consider reading a text that is designed to provide an overview, such as a textbook or one of the legal encyclopedias (see the reading list in Appendix I).

You can approach your research by dividing it into three stages: gaining an overview, focusing on the topic, and looking at primary sources to find supporting details. The basic idea is to start simply and broadly, and gradually narrow in on the detail you will discuss. However, be warned that this suggested approach won't suit all essays.

As you read, be sure to keep notes of what you read, your response to it, and how you think it may fit into your essay (even if you aren't sure how your essay is going to look).

Overview—textbooks and encyclopedias

In the overview stage, your aim is to get a broad picture of your area of inquiry. This is best achieved by looking at a variety of sources (often just skimming them if they are confirming what you already know). These will include:

Your textbook
It is astounding the number of people who will commence reading cases for an essay without first seeing how the textbook deals with the subject. Even though the textbook may only spend a few pages (or paragraphs) on your topic, this will give you a context from which to begin your more in-depth reading.

Note the distinction between textbooks and casebooks. Casebooks provide excerpts of other materials and are less helpful in providing a concise summary of an area of law. In fact, that is really your task: you are meant to identify the principles through your reading.

Remember too that it is precisely the simplicity of textbooks that limits their use. It is normally inappropriate to refer to a textbook in your final essay if there is some other authority (such as a case).

Other textbooks
Look at the brief discussion of your topic in other textbooks in your library. (Often the best are kept together in the reserve section.) You need only skim the text if it is repeating what you know, but this will help you gain a sense of common ways of dealing with the subject. (But don't feel that you must conform with these views!)

Legal encyclopedias, such as *Laws of Australia* or *Halsbury's Laws of Australia*
Legal encyclopedias are another useful source of general information. Again, these services attempt to simplify the law—though in this case for practitioners more than students. The loose-leaf encyclopedias are particularly useful because they will be more up-to-date than most textbooks.

Focus—journal articles, law reform commission reports...

Now it's time to look at resources that focus more on your topic. Normally, the overview stage will have proved helpful in identifying issues and key words that will make your research easier. At this stage, your plan should be growing quite detailed.

Using these key words, search for articles on a computer database (make sure you know how everything works in your library; maybe go for a tour in your first week). Try limiting or expanding your search until you have found a few key articles that you will read. Keep a list of all the articles that may be relevant, and rank them in terms of their importance. Be warned that many of the articles on these databases appear in United States law reviews. On many topics, such articles will be less relevant than those in Australian, United Kingdom, Canadian and New Zealand journals.

When reading the articles, try beginning with the most recent, as it will probably refer to earlier works. Don't forget

Detail—primary materials (cases, legislation, reports . . .)

Once you have mapped out the broad area of your inquiry and developed a basic understanding of some of the issues that it raises, it is time to start looking at the primary materials. These will normally form the central core of the substantive legal research of your essay, but delaying them until this stage will focus your reading on their importance to you.

If you are looking at case law, by now you should be aware of the 'major' cases in the area you are considering, and how some commentators view them. As with the journal articles, rank the cases you want to look at in terms of their importance, and look at them in that order.

Skimming the headnote of a case will help you establish its relevance. Many cases deal with a variety of issues, only a few of which may be of interest to you.

Similarly, consider skimming a digest such as the *Australian Legal Digest*. Such publications present brief summaries of cases and are useful if you have a long list of cases to consider. This will save you time finding all the cases, whilst directing you to other cases on the same subject. This is also an opportunity to further update your work by using the *Australian Legal Monthly Digest*.

Cross-check: *See also Chapter 6, 'Reading Case Law'.*

WRITING YOUR ESSAY

Planning and drafting

Planning how to set out your essay and writing the first draft are activities that usually follow your research. You have collected the information and formulated a point of view about the topic. Your task now is to present the material in such a way that both the evidence (information you have collected during your research) and argument (the perspective you are bringing to the topic) are clear to the reader. You need a good framework and a logical structure for all of this material.

Later-year students who have become quite practised at essay writing often begin writing while they are researching. Drafting paragraphs as they collect information and reflect on it helps them to expedite the writing process. For a start, though, you may prefer to separate these activities.

When you are planning an essay draft, identify a suitable structure and write the essay draft in sections. For example, all essays require an introduction, a main body, and a conclusion. The main body of the essay is where most of your effort is required, and it's a good idea to write sections of the main body before you attempt the introduction or conclusion.

While writing essays for law subjects is similar to writing other essays (i.e. you need to plan your approach, structure an argument, present information clearly and concisely), the most important differences that often cause trouble for students are the use of authority and the law student's bugbear: the footnote.

CITING AUTHORITY

Before considering how to cite authority, it is important to understand why you need to cite material. There are four main reasons: to show that your discussion is based on other people's ideas; to support a proposition of your own; to relate your work to existing scholarship; and to qualify statements in the text. We'll show you below how this citation of authority is done; footnoting is the convention in legal writing.

Other people's ideas

As in non-legal writing, references commonly indicate the use of another person's ideas. If you take an idea or a quote without properly acknowledging the author's contribution to your work, this is a form of plagiarism—a sort of academic theft.

Citing an idea or a quote

The impartiality of the judge him or herself is generally taken for granted, just as it has been assumed for almost as long as there have been judges that years of practice as a barrister are the only qualifications needed for judicial office.[1] Training judges to be fully human, to develop the 'special ability to listen with connection'[2] is doubly difficult when the establishment view is that no training is necessary at all.

1 Michael Kirby, *The Judges* (1983) 24.
2 Cain, 'Good and Bad Bias: A Comment on Feminist Theory and Judging' (1988) 61 *Southern California Law Review* 1945, 1954.

Support for a proposition

The most important and specifically legal use of citation is in justifying a statement about the law. If you write that courts have traditionally not imposed a legal duty to rescue, you should cite a case that states this principle of law. In particular, you should cite the most authoritative case in point. Where available, this will mean the most recent High Court authority, which should be cited first. Other cases and secondary materials (such as books, journal articles) may be cited afterwards.

> **Example: Authority for a proposition**
> Courts will not generally recognise a duty to rescue.[3]
>
> ---
> 3   *Jaensch v Coffey* (1984) 155 CLR 549, 578 (Deane J). See also *Hargrave v Goldman* (1963) 11-CLR 40, 65-6 (Windeyer J); *Dorset Yacht Co Ltd v Home Office* [1970] AC 1004, 1060 (Lord Diplock).

Relating your work to existing scholarship

Another legal convention—with its origins perhaps in US law reviews—is to use footnotes simply to position your essay in relation to the existing scholarship. Rather than acknowledging the contribution of these articles to your own, the purpose is simply to show that you are aware of them.

This use of footnotes is often criticised as adding nothing to your essay. If you are worried that your footnotes look 'light'—or, more importantly, do not reflect the amount of research you have done—you may want to consider it. If there is an article you have read which is relevant but is not included in the footnotes, see if it would be appropriate to refer to it at a point in your essay where you discuss a similar point, and use the 'cf' introductory signal (discussed below).

Qualifying statements in the text

Finally, footnotes can be used to briefly qualify broad statements in the text.

This does not mean that you can simply cut from the text and paste into the footnotes. Most examiners are awake to such attempts to avoid word limits.

The basic rule is that you should be able to read the entire essay without having to refer to the footnotes at all. If the text does not make sense without the footnotes, you are probably relying too much on your reader jumping from text to footnotes and back.

USING FOOTNOTES

Footnotes should present all information necessary to locate references. They should be succinct, consistent and as clear as possible. Uniformity and ease of retrieval are the goals. This section looks at three aspects of footnotes:

- the introductory signal that indicates their uses
- basic methods of citation for commonly used materials, and
- multiple references to the same work.

Introductory signals—'see', 'cf', 'contra'

These signals indicate the way in which you are using the footnote.

Where a reference is used as direct authority (whether to acknowledge an idea, or support a proposition of law), there is no need to use a signal.

Where a reference is used as more general support for an argument, 'see' or 'see, e.g.' should be used. Where a work is included for additional or background material, 'see generally' should be used.

When you are comparing your ideas with other works, 'cf' (*confer:* compare with) should be used. The work being cited is not authority for the proposition or argument, but provides a useful comparison. When you are contradicting another work, 'contra' should be used. Use this if you disagree with the view of an author or a judge. This is the least commonly used signal, especially by students.

Basic citation methods

It is not possible to provide an exhaustive list of citation methods. However, we will give you the basic rules of thumb. The model used here is the *Melbourne University Law Review Style Guide*, which should be referred to for more detailed information.

i Cases

> 13 *Commonwealth v Tasmania* (1983) 158 CLR 1 ('Dams Case').
> 14 *Thwaites v Ryan* [1984] VR 65. Dams Case (1983) 158 CLR 1, 35.

Note that square brackets [ ] are used for law reports in which the year indicates the volume being cited. Round brackets ( ) are used where the year is not an integral part of the citation.

ii Periodicals

> 26 Sir Anthony Mason, 'A Bill of Rights for Australia?' (1989) 5 *Australian Bar Review* 79, 81.
>
> 27 Rosemary Mnookin and Leone Kornhauser, 'Bargaining in the Shadow of the Law: The Case of Divorce' (1979) 88 *Yale Law Journal* 950.

iii Books

> 38 Jürgen Habermas, *Toward a Rational Society* (1971) 45.

iv Statutes and the Constitution

> 49 Australia Act 1986 (Cth).
> 50 Trustee Act 1928 (Vic) s 10.
> 51 Australian Constitution s 51(xxix).

v Newspapers

> 62 Pamela Smith, 'Allende Had It Coming', *The Sun* (Sydney), 30 March 1974, 4.
> 63 Editorial, 'The Cost of Democracy', *The Age* (Melbourne), 18 July 1993.

vi Official papers, parliamentary debates

> 74 Victoria, *Parliamentary Debates, Legislative Assembly*, 23 October 1968, 1197.
> 75 Commonwealth, *Hansard, House of Representatives*, 1 June 1977, 2294-5.
> 76 Australian Law Reform Commission, *Sentencing: Penalties*, Discussion Paper No 30 (1987) para 286.

vii Other references

For citation methods for specific legal materials (such as international law), see your relevant Style Guide.

In all cases, remember that uniformity and ease of

WRITING LAW ESSAYS

retrieval are the goals. Author(s), title, date of publication and page reference are generally the necessary core of the reference.

Multiple references to the same work

After the first occasion, a citation should not be repeated in full but written as briefly as possible, referring back to the footnote in which the full citation may be found.

i Ibid

If the citation is

- in the immediately preceding footnote, and
- is the only citation in that footnote

then it is appropriate to use 'Ibid', which means 'in the same place'.

> 5 *Mabo v State of Queensland* [No 2] (1992) 175 CLR 1 ('Mabo').
> 6 Ibid 7.
> 7 Jürgen Habermas, *Toward a Rational Society* (1971) 74.
> 8 Ibid.
> 9 Mabo (1992) 175 CLR 1, 72.

ii Above n x

On other occasions, references other than cases may be cited by the author's name, and a reference to the footnote with the full citation. For example, if you wish to refer the reader to Habermas again (in the above example in the footnote numbered 7), you simply write 'above n 7'. This means 'see footnote 7 given previously for full details'.

Multiple references to cases must continue to use their full citation, but the name of the case may be abbreviated (e.g. 'Mabo', 'Dams case', etc).

> 10 Habermas, above n 7, 74.
> 11 Ibid.
> 12 Mabo (1992) 175 CLR 1, 69.
> 13 Habermas, above n 7, 110.

Hints

One way to speed up the referencing process is to keep a list of the complete citations of all the references you are using (especially those you are using more than once). Next to them, make a list of abbreviations, as shown in Figure 8.1.

| HAB71 | Jürgen Habermas, *Toward a Rational Society* (1971) |
| MAB092 | *Mabo v State of Queensland* [No 2] (1992) 175 CLR 1 ('Mabo') |

Figure 8.1: Example abbreviations and full citations

As you write your essay, just type the abbreviation in the footnotes on each occasion that you use the reference. Then, when you are finished editing the text, go through and systematically replace the abbreviations. On the first occasion, copy the whole reference. On the second and subsequent occasions, use the appropriate form of citation for multiple references.

To ensure that a cross-reference does not have to be manually changed each time you add in a footnote that changes the numbering, some word-processing packages enable you to use cross-reference fields that update automatically. Learn how to use these, as they simplify the footnoting process considerably.

A POSTSCRIPT—THE COMPUTER AGE

Most universities have computer labs for those students who do not have their own personal computer. This is to ensure that students who cannot afford the latest technology, or those who do not have suitable living arrangements, are not penalised. However, be aware that there will be limited access to such labs and that the demand will be heavy when assessments are due. Though it may take a little organisation and time management to make use of the lab, you will find that you need to prepare your assignments through word processing (this is in keeping with the professional standards expected of student work at university level). Alternatively, you may like to consider getting a low-cost student loan to enable you to purchase your own computer.

PREPARING FOR LAW EXAMS

> We are all, it seems, saving ourselves for the Senior Prom. But many of us forget that somewhere along the way we must learn to dance.
>
> Alan Harrington

Studying for an open book law exam is very different from studying for exams at school or in other faculties. This chapter outlines some of the important things to keep in mind while preparing for law exams. It uses negligence as an example, but the principles we demonstrate can also be applied more generally with other examples from the field of law.

WHAT IS BEING TESTED?

Understanding, reasoning, evaluating

The purpose of a law exam is not to test whether you have *memorised* the law, but whether you can *understand* and *use* the law.

This is why we have open book exams—the examination is not to test your memory, but your ability to pick relevant issues and apply legal principles that you have studied during the year. Of course you do have to 'know' which cases are important, which doctrine is favoured and so on. However, in general the most difficult aspect of a law exam is working out how to apply these cases and doctrines to new circumstances, such as hypothetical problems.

Therefore, a crucial step in preparing for a law exam is developing a familiarity with the material being studied, and an understanding of how the individual cases fit together in the area of law being studied.

Once you have a basic understanding of the subject material, it is then a matter of demonstrating that you can reason, using the case law and legislation, and evaluate the likely outcome in particular circumstances.

This chapter discusses how to approach an 'open book' exam and preparing notes that are 'exam friendly'.

head in the Case

OPEN BOOK EXAMS

Making your notes count

'Open book' means that you can take into your exam virtually anything short of a computer database and mobile phone. It is tempting to take into the examination every piece of written material you have received or created during the year. If you actually have to read much during the exam, however, then you have not prepared adequately and will be wasting valuable time that could be spent writing. (Having said that, there is no harm taking in things such as notes, summaries, texts, casebooks, etc.—just in case—but you should not expect to be looking at much of it.)

During the year, what you should be focusing on is preparing notes that are useful.

STUDYING LAW AT UNIVERSITY

This does not merely mean summaries. The whole point of 'open book' exams is that they enable you to do much of the work before entering the exam hall. What you should be preparing are brief, concise notes on the doctrines being tested.

Beware of two things in particular:

- Doing no work. You are kidding yourself if you think you can rely exclusively on someone else's notes. Aside from the simple fact that they may have made mistakes, notes cannot possibly encapsulate all necessary information. Good notes are intended to 'jog' your memory, to draw your mind to other connections. Remember that making notes involves thinking, synthesising, analysing, and evaluation. For this reason, notes are very personal. It may, however, be worth borrowing a couple of other students' notes for comparison: to see how they have approached the task of condensing the course.
- Doing too much 'busy' work. On the other hand, you should resist the temptation to prepare endless summaries. Summarise the course as much as you think is necessary, but when you are actually sitting in the exam hall, ten pages will always be better than 100. No matter how much you take into the exam, it will be no use unless you can find the relevant section quickly. You need to be familiar with your material and be able to access information quickly from any relevant sections.

A system that often works well is to have longer notes accompanied by a summary with brief statements of the law and relevant cases, with references to the page numbers in your more detailed notes. You could also colour code related summaries and detailed notes, or perhaps use sticky notes to mark relevant places.

In addition, you can include brief critical comments on the law that you are applying (such as the application of the reasonable person test for breach). To this end, you may wish to incorporate one- or two-sentence comments in your notes that may provide the basis for such critique, without slowing you down in the exam.

EXAM-FRIENDLY NOTES

'Just the facts, ma'am?'

Case summaries are useful as a learning aid, but not when you are sitting in the exam hall. Concentrating on 'just the facts' will not necessarily serve you as well as you think. When preparing your notes for the end of year exam, you have to keep in mind that their purpose is not simply to remind you of the facts of cases, but to enable you to apply principles of law to new circumstances.

Translating historical knowledge into instrumental knowledge

One of your first tasks in preparing notes for an exam is the process of translating your historical understanding of cases (what happened, what the judges said) into instrumental knowledge—that is, you have to turn fact-specific case law into principles that may be applied generally.

> **Example: Donoghue v Stevenson**
> What is important here is not that if a snail makes its way into a bottle of ginger beer, then the manufacturer is going to have to pay for the injured party's gastroenteritis. Instead, you should understand that this was the case that established the 'neighbour' principle, by which negligence was extended as a cause of action applicable not only to those with whom one has a contractual or direct relationship, but to those persons who are 'so closely and directly affected' by your actions that you ought reasonably to have them in your contemplation.

GETTING AN OVERVIEW

One reason why exams are favoured as a method of assessment is that they force you to develop an overview of the course. For example, to do well in a subject on the topic of negligence, it is vital that you understand the function that negligence serves and how each part (duty, breach, causation/remoteness and damages) fits together. The tort of negligence may appear merely to be a steeplechase, but its separate parts serve distinct functions.

Duty, for example, is in part a threshold test for a negligence action, but it also represents the extent to which the law is prepared to hold people accountable for their actions. The question of 'who is my neighbour' is thus answered by resolving the tension between foreseeability and proximity, with policy operating as a check on this tension. The relationship between these concepts is shown diagrammatically in Figure 9.1 below.

Foreseeability		**Proximity**
the potential for harm to others	*restricted by*	*limits on individual responsibility*

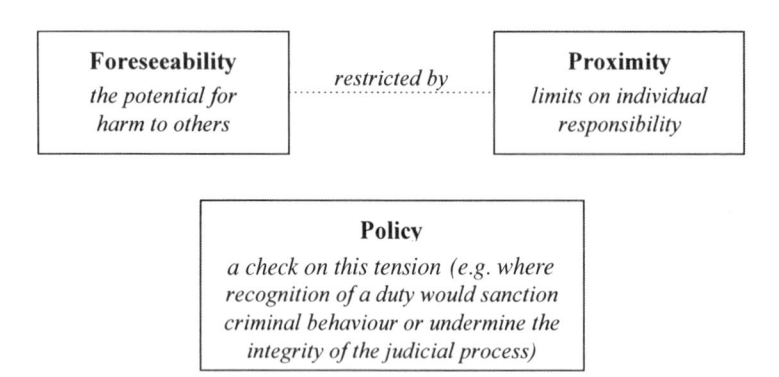

Policy
a check on this tension (e.g. where recognition of a duty would sanction criminal behaviour or undermine the integrity of the judicial process)

Figure 9.1: Concepts to be considered with regard to 'duty'

Thinking of the course in broad terms such as this is crucial to making sense of what you are doing. Once you can see the 'big picture'—negligence as a regime of fault-based loss-shifting, as well as a normative regime of individual

PREPARING FOR LAW EXAMS

responsibility—then the individual pieces themselves will make more sense.

Start large, then sharpen the focus

In writing an answer to a hypothetical problem, you should start with the issues to be considered and the legal principles that are important, before dealing in more detail with specific problems that arise in the case. In addition, you cannot simply approach all problems the same way. If you are dealing with a situation where a primary school student injured during a class is bringing an action against her teacher, it is highly unlikely that duty will be an issue—say as much and then move on.

As a result, your notes should enable you to see the 'big picture' and move easily between issues. Following in Figure 9.2 is an example of notes that do this. Again, we consider the question of duty.

TRAINING FOR THE EVENT

Timed writing

> From writing rapidly it does not result that one writes well, but from writing well it results that one writes rapidly.
> Quintillian, AD95 (translated by Clyde Murley)

Part of your preparation for exams of any kind should include training yourself to perform the task that you will need to do during the exam. For example, it's a good idea to practise timed writing for law exams, even open book exams. See just how much you can get down on paper within a certain time, counting searching through your notes, making the response legible, and polishing the final product. This is the best way to use past papers. It is not essential

STUDYING LAW AT UNIVERSITY

Duty of care
- any binding precedent/accepted position?
- if not, apply Deane's 3-stage test:
- foreseeability of some kind of harm to pl or class of persons including pl if def fails to take care
- 'so closely and directly affected': Donoghue (1932, HL)
- proximity: a limit on liability, class of plaintiffs
- physical, circumstantial, or causal
- developed in Jaensch, adopted in Cook, used (by all but Dawson J) in Gala
- policy (?? separate from proximity?)
- government policy decisions: Sutherland SC
- duty of lawyers to the court: Giannarelli
- joint illegality: Gala
- particular situations
- omissions (pp. 39-40)
- duty to do sth only arises when statute imposes (e.g. police) or as in Hargrave v Goldman (per Brennan J in Sutherland SC); special duty to neighbour's property, depends on def's capabilities
- controlling conduct of others (pp. 40-2)
- ...
- personal non-delegable duty (pp. 50)
- ...
- nervous shock (pp. 6-7)
- ...
- intermediate inspection (p. 37)
- intervening act only prevents liability if def is relying on that intervention to pick up defects (Voli)

Figure 9.2: Sample exam study notes on the topic of 'duty'

to sit working on the old exam for the entire two or three hours; do sections or questions in the relevant time. (And remember to try it with no coffee, music, or mobile phone!)

Another good preparation activity is to write very full,

detailed answers to a couple of questions, just to make sure of the extent of your understanding of the topic. You can then practise answering the same question in the allotted time, having reminded yourself of the important issues.

Fit for the test

Consider some other issues during your exam preparation: are you training yourself to be at your most mentally alert between 2 a.m. and 4 a.m.? How many university exams are held at that time? Certainly you need to put in more hours around exam time, but make sure you don't diminish your mental and physical capabilities by fatiguing yourself senselessly.

Any little time is a good time

Make better use of small amounts of time as the academic year dashes towards its conclusion. Repeated small sessions with your notes can be just as—if not more—effective than those endless hours doing 'desk time' when you are really thinking about something else. Doing a little bit often is the secret to becoming familiar with any material, and familiarity with your notes will be your most valuable asset during an open book exam.

Keep in mind the natural law: 'Reality bites'

> The word 'now' is like a bomb through the window, and it ticks.
>
> Arthur Miller

The exams will come around sooner than you think. Swot vac and the end of semester are no time to indulge your perfectionism. Similarly, this is no time to berate yourself for all those missed classes and all that time spent on X (see Chapter 3, Myth No. 5). Be realistic, but also be kind to yourself: what's done is done, and you need to make the best of where you are now. Remember your past successes; reduce panic and negative feelings, keep up a healthy lifestyle. Most importantly, concentrate on what you have a grasp of and build your knowledge from there.

LEARN TO USE THE LAW

Studying law is ultimately about learning to use it. This means identifying relevant issues, applying old principles to new facts, and above all reasoning legally. This chapter has provided a guide to what you can do to prepare yourself for the open book, hypothetical-based exams in law. Points you should keep in mind are:

- Preparing notes that are 'exam-friendly'. This will generally mean a brief summary, accompanied by more detailed notes on particular areas of the course.
- Getting an overview of the course. It is much easier to apply law to particular situations or hypothetical cases if you understand the broader social purposes that it is meant to serve.

Most of the work for an exam like this is done before you step into the exam hall. In order to check how you are going, however, it is vital that you practise using the law. This means:

- Sitting practice exams. If possible, get a teacher/lecturer to correct your exam, or talk over the answers (later) with a fellow student. Even if this is not possible it is worth doing the practice, if only to see how to allocate time to work on different areas of the course.

PREPARING FOR LAW EXAMS

- Doing practical problems. You will do some in class, but others may be found in some of the textbooks available from your library.
- Thinking critically about the cases that you read. There is not a great deal of difference between a judge making a ruling in a case and a student sitting a hypothetical exam, so consider how judges approach novel problems in law.

In the next chapter we consider what happens in the exam hall.

10 SITTING LAW EXAMS

> A sudden, bold, and unexpected question doth many times surprise a man and lay him open.
> Francis Bacon, 1625

Open book exams with hypothetical problems are a crucial part of studying law. However, there are also law exams that ask you to answer essay questions. In this chapter we discuss how to approach such an exam, from reading time and planning through to presenting your answer in words.

Examples are drawn from many subjects and we hope they will be of assistance to students of all levels. (Note that this chapter discusses 'ideal' answers. Don't worry if you can't do everything suggested here.)

DIVIDE AND CONQUER

This chapter divides the exam into four stages:

- the issues stage: reading time
- the planning stage: the basic format
- the structuring stage: using the law
- the writing stage: answers that attract marks.

SITTING LAW EXAMS

THE ISSUES STAGE: READING TIME

Facts, issues and cases

It's time now to start thinking about how to approach a hypothetical problem in an exam question. You basically understand what the course is about, you have your notes, and now you are confronted with a new facts situation.

The exam as a whole

Reading time is a crucial part of the exam. Often, it will start 30 minutes before the exam proper commences—so be on time!

You should already know what the format of the exam is (i.e. how many sections, how many questions from each section, whether they are hypotheticals, essays), but use the first minute of reading time to check that you know exactly what is required of you. Getting a decent mark is hard enough—don't be the person who only answers two-thirds of the assessable questions and thus has to get H1s to pass!

Similarly, you should go in with a clear idea of how much time you have on each question. Rather than simply allocating x minutes to each question, write down the exact time frame for each question, as we show in Figure 10.1.

Example time schedule for two hour exam starting at 2:15pm with ½ hr reading time	
1:45–1:50	Skim entire paper, deciding which questions to do—note major issues in margin
1:50–2:05	Read and make notes on question from Part A (40 marks)
2:05–2:15	Read and make notes on question from Part B (30 marks)
2:15–3:20	Start writing answer to Part A
3:20–4:10	Start writing answer to Part B
4:10–4:15	Review entire paper
4:15	Exam ends

Figure 10.1: Example time schedule for two hour exam starting at 2:15p.m. with 30 minutes reading time

If you have a choice of questions, decide quickly which questions you are going to attempt. It is often a good idea to do the question you think that you will do best first. This both inspires confidence and enables the other 90% of your brain to keep working on the other questions.

Finally, it is absolutely vital that you attempt all the required questions. Don't sit staring vaguely, wondering where your answer can possibly go from the point to which you have taken it. Go on to another section, and worry about un-painting yourself out of that corner later. Remember that it will always be easier to get the first half of the allocated marks on any particular question than the second half, so go on to the next question and see if you can spend the time usefully there.

Read the question

It may sound basic, but many students do themselves a disservice by failing to use their reading time efficiently. In most law exams, the first half hour is designed to stop you jumping straight into a written answer.

You should consider this time as the issues stage, where you are mentally planning your answer.

Look for issues that arise from the facts (remembering that these 'facts' are a story to put the legal positions and consequences into context). It is rare for examiners to include 'red herrings' to distract you. Look at all the information you are given and as you read each sentence, think: 'What issue does this raise?' Mark the issues in the margin or on a separate sheet of notepaper. Do this as the ideas hit you, as they may not on a second reading.

As you read the facts, think about other cases you have read or discussed during the year. Different points in hypotheticals will often relate closely to cases studied in the course. Write the name of the cases down as you read the problem.

Watch out for clues, and beware of jumping too quickly

on an idea. For example, if the facts state that 'A, using all due care, carried B to the hospital', this means that you need not discuss A's liability in negligence for injuries to B as a result of this act, or perhaps merely say why you do not need to do so.

> For every human problem, there is a neat, simple solution; and it is always wrong.
>
> Mencken's Metalaw

Of course, your first idea may be right! However, whether you think you can dive straight into the answer or whether you're totally confused, it may be useful to pause and look over another question, to allow yourself to digest the facts. Then come back to the first question and plan your answer to it.

THE PLANNING STAGE: THE BASIC FORMAT

Who, what, how

> He who asks questions cannot avoid the answers.
>
> Proverb from the Cameroons

A basic structure for planning your answer to any legal problem is to ask yourself three simple questions: Who are the parties to the dispute? What do they want? How could they get what they want using the law I have studied? This is the planning stage of your answer, and will also take place in reading time (at least for the first question).

Who are the parties?

Identifying parties is a threshold stage of the exam. In the great tradition of the *X-Files*, the basic idea here is to suspect everyone. Each person discussed in the problem is a possible plaintiff/victim and/or defendant, or perhaps a mere device to complete the story. Read the problem with this in mind (and remember that the answer is out there, somewhere).

Abbreviate the names of the parties. Usually, it is enough to write the first letter of a party's name to identify them. Often, this will make sense in the context of the problem (Priscilla the Plaintiff, Delia the Defendant, Victor the Victim, or Albert, Barry and Celia).

Try out the combinations. Make a list of everyone who has suffered injury in the hypothetical and see which of the other parties could conceivably be held legally responsible for that injury.

Re-read the question. If you are told to discuss only the liability of one defendant, or the civil action of one plaintiff, of course don't waste time on irrelevancies. Be particularly careful here where one party is an employee or agent of another. Similarly, watch out for restrictions on the actions to be discussed, or even on issues to be considered within an action.

We have made an example list of the characters involved in an imaginary case in Figure 10.2.

What do they want?

Still in the planning stage, consider what each of your injured parties may want. Sometimes this will be simple, as in the case of a common law action in negligence where the only remedy is damages, or in criminal law where a fine or imprisonment are the major possibilities. In contract, damages or specific performance may be an option (but note that specific performance is discretionary). Some other situations may be more complex. A property law example is given in Figure 10.3.

SITTING LAW EXAMS

> **Example: Negligence**
>
> Be particularly careful in situations where a person may be acting for an employer. Consider the possibility that an injured plaintiff could sue
> - the individual who caused her injury
> - her employer vicariously, and/or
> - her employer directly under a direct non-delegable duty (see *Introvigne*)
>
> ```
>                    Derek (employee) --vicariously-- Acme Ltd (employer)
>                         (1)                              (2)
>   P (injured)
>                         (3)
>                    Acme (employer)  sued directly for breach of non-delegable duty
> ```

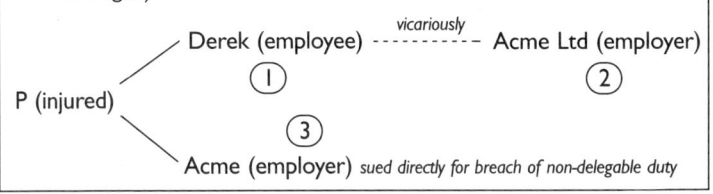

Figure 10.2: Characters in a negligence case

> **Example: Property Law**
>
> In Property Law, a variety of remedies may be possible arising from a dispute over land, including:
> - a legal interest in the land
> - an equitable interest in the land, such as a constructive trust
> - compensation under s 110 of the Transfer of Land Act

Figure 10.3: Some remedies to consider in property law

How can they get it?

Consider all possible causes of action. Even if something seems far-fetched, it is worth raising the cause of action even if you dismiss it in the same sentence. In a negligence action, watch out for any breach of statutory duty action that could be run in the alternative—and look at all the possible defendants to each action. Watch for statutory actions or limitations on common law claims. Figure 10.4 gives an example from Constitutional & Administrative Law.

Note that if you have a number of possible defendants to similar causes of action, it is perfectly acceptable to write in relation to B, 'as for the action against A with the

> **Example: Constitutional and Administrative Law**
>
> Always watch out for cases that might involve both constitutional and administrative issues. For example, if a State Act requires newspaper proprietors to pay a licence fee and M is denied a licence, what she wants is not necessarily to have the legislation struck down—her goal is to continue running her business. This may be achieved in two ways:
>
> - ensuring she gets a licence under the Act—perhaps through an administrative law action if there has been any impropriety, and/or
> - removing the need for a licence—here considering the possibility of striking down the Act, perhaps because it is an excise (Constitution, s 90).

Figure 10.4: Some causes of action in Constitutional and Administrative Law

following differences'. This can be repeated for C and so on. The same applies to problems with multiple plaintiffs.

THE STRUCTURING STAGE: USING THE LAW

Issues, tests and alternatives

The final stage of your planning lies in finalising the issues to be discussed under the cause(s) of action you have identified against the defendant(s): this is the structuring stage. From your focused reading of the question, you should have identified most of the issues, but always keep your eyes open for a new issue that may leap up at you as you work through your answer.

It is important to structure your answer logically. If you are arguing in the alternative, make this clear and use headings to break up your answer. Using headings also makes your structure easier to follow, and removes the need for you to waste time writing connecting phrases such as 'I will now discuss X'.

In addition, keep the following points in mind:

SITTING LAW EXAMS

- What is the precise act or omission that the plaintiff is saying was wrongful? (e.g. in TPL, what is the breach?) Note that there may be more than one, or different wrongful acts or omissions for different defendants. What are the causal connections (note the plural) between each of the allegedly wrongful acts and the harm suffered?
- What tests will establish the defendant's liability for the alleged wrongful act? Use your notes to determine what the plaintiff will have to prove in order to obtain her remedy against the defendant.
- What is the effect if a test is not satisfied? If a plaintiff cannot satisfy one of the tests, will this mean her action fails? (Normally argue in the alternative if it does.) Or is there another argument that she can make?
- A key skill in answering a hypothetical is knowing how much time to spend on each issue. Reading the problem as a whole should give you an idea of the issues that need to be addressed.
- Are there any defences available to the defendant?

THE WRITING STAGE: ANSWERS THAT ATTRACT MARKS

> I always do the first line well, but I have trouble doing the others.
> Moliere, 1659 (translated by Donald Frame)

Issues, principles and the facts

Be wary of 'discussing' the law too much in a hypothetical. Your *reasoning* skills are being tested, not your memory or your powers as a storyteller, and so there is no point wasting time discussing the history of the cause of action being used.

Avoid the temptation to quote extensively. Normally only a few words need to be cited—"far-fetched or fanciful' (*Wyong*)', or "common sense' (*March*)'. Nor should you paraphrase much of the cases you are discussing: what is being tested is the application of the principles, not your ability to describe the case.

In general, try not to think of this as an essay—it is more akin to a maths problem with commentary. With this in mind, have a look at Figure 10.5 for the basic structure of discussing any hypothetical. Also bear in mind that some questions will require greater depth on particular issues.

> **Example format**
> Who is suing whom in what area of law?
> What are the main issues to discuss? List the major hurdles to proving the cause of action, then discuss them in a logical order.
>
> Issue 1: What is the relevant principle (or the appropriate test)? A brief statement in the abstract as to the broad position of the law, perhaps applied directly to the facts. (Cite the leading case as authority in brackets.)
>
> Do the facts show that the plaintiff clearly falls inside or outside the principle? Apply the facts to the principle/test you have identified.
>
> If the plaintiff clearly falls inside the test, move on to more 'interesting' (i.e. valuable) issues.
>
> If the answer is less clear, what would need to be argued in order to resolve the issue? Is there any other authority that would assist either party? State briefly what the plaintiff would argue. Discuss how the defendant would respond:
>
> 'A would argue that it was not "far-fetched or fanciful" (Wyong) that... In response, B would question what ought to have been foreseen at that time, bearing in mind the lack of any industry-wide knowledge of the risk (Roe).'
>
> Make a swift decision as to which argument would be accepted. Then move on to the next issue.

Figure 10.5: A basic structure for discussing a hypothetical

EXAM PARAGRAPHS—ARE THEY HELPFUL?

It is often possible to prepare 'exam paragraphs' that are concise statements of the law or a test that is applicable

SITTING LAW EXAMS

any time you discuss the issue. *Beware though of using exam paragraphs as a substitute for thinking.* Using sentences from paragraphs you have prepared from last year's papers (often available on reserve in the library) without careful consideration may cause you to bypass important issues.

> Writing comes more easily if you have something to say.
> Sholem Asch

Sometimes this will be useful in presenting basic information briefly, as shown in Figure 10.6 below.

Example: Negligence—basic plan

In order to succeed in a negligence action, [P] must establish that
(i) a duty of care was owed to her by [D];
(ii) that [D] breached that duty by [.....];
(iii) that the breach in so far as it was wrongful caused [P's damage] which was not too remote; and
(iv) no defences operate to assist [D].

Figure 10.6: A basic plan for an exam paragraph on negligence

Note, however, that it is usually better to introduce the issues and demonstrate a sophisticated understanding of the problem from the outset, as Figure 10.7 shows.

Example: Negligence—sophisticated plan

Of the three elements required to prove a negligence action (duty, breach, causation: Jaensch), P's greatest hurdle will be to establish that
(i) D failed to take the precautions expected of a reasonable person (breach); and that
(ii) A's actions do not sever the "causal chain" (March) connecting D's act and P's injury.
Duty of care is non-problematic—clearly coming within Deane's test in Jaensch.

Figure 10.7: A more detailed exam paragraph on negligence

STUDYING LAW AT UNIVERSITY

Exam paragraphs can be useful in a contested area of law, because they can help you to think about the issues. Whenever a teacher or a textbook highlights an area of law as uncertain, you should prepare yourself for a question on precisely that area. Just such an intriguing area is given in the example exam paragraph shown in Figure 10.8.

Example: Contract—silence as a misrepresentation

'Even mere silence may amount to a misrepresentation if the silence is intentional: Henjo

Silence was not enough to invoke s 52 in Rhone-Poulenc (1986 Fed Ct FC), the distinction appearing to be that a deliberate decision to remain silent is required. Clearly, where this amounts to a positive act it is 'misleading conduct' in the sense of the Act, or may be unconscionable within the meaning of Part IVA of the TPA

The Fed Ct FC followed this line of reasoning in Henjo (1988) where it held that the failure to inform a buyer that current profits were dependent on breaking liquor licensing regulations was 'misleading conduct'

The application of s 52 to 'silence' does not depend on the existence of a particular relationship (as does common law misrep) but rather is determined by reference to all the circs of the case (Henjo)

Figure 10.8: An exam paragraph based on a contested area of law

Note that this section of the notes is broken into parts which may be used separately. This is important as the amount you write will depend on how important the issue is to the problem at hand.

You may also want to use this technique to introduce brief critical comments on the law that you are applying (e.g. discussing the gendered nature of the 'reasonable man/person' test in negligence). These should be kept brief, as you are being tested on your application of the doctrine, but occasionally policy arguments will be of greater importance. (As for example, when dealing with the question of whether proximity is anything more than a mask for policy.)

FILLING IN THE GAPS

Unless they manage to steal a copy of the exam paper before the test, however (NOT a recommended course of action!), a good examination will force all students to think creatively about the law they have studied. Often this means you will be confronted with issues that you might not have expected, or don't quite know how to relate to what you have studied.

In such situations it is vital that you do not panic. Keep the following points in mind:

- Trust the reading guide: The examination is designed to test only what you have studied in the course—be confident that something you have looked at will be relevant.
- Trust the examiners: Examiners rarely introduce red herrings to confuse students—more often than not, something which appears out of the blue is simply a new way of looking at an old problem. (This is particularly true of property law, with the variety of interests that may be discussed in an exam.)
- Trust yourself: Even if you feel completely lost, reduce the facts to the most basic principles of the area of law addressed by the question—relate them to the policy that lies behind the doctrine and discuss the issues from such 'first principles'.

Write quickly, but don't write waffle. Think about the examiners reading your answer: will they put a tick next to the sentence you are writing right now? Or are you filling up the page with vague, multi-purpose information that fails to demonstrate how well you know the principles of the law?

DON'T PANIC!

The single most important piece of advice that can be given to anyone preparing for a law exam is to sit practice exams. No amount of reading, no amount of notetaking can compare to the experience of actually sitting down in exam conditions and seeing how well you can identify issues, plan an answer, and structure a discussion of the law as it relates to a given facts situation.

Talk over a problem with your classmates, write an answer on your own without time constraints, then try a couple with time constraints. This will help you practise answering questions and allotting appropriate time for each aspect. Ask your teacher if she can look over a sample answer you have written.

In this chapter we have provided basic advice to help you prepare for exams that include hypothetical problems. In particular, we have suggested that a useful way of approaching any problem is through dividing up your time to ask yourself the following questions:

What issues are raised in the facts situation? Read each sentence and think: What are the legal implications of this sentence? Try to recall cases dealing with similar facts (note that there will usually be some distinguishing features).

Who are the parties, what do they want, how can they get it? How should you plan your answer? Are you asked to 'Advise Paula' or 'Discuss the issues'? In any case, remember to discuss both sides (always in the third person and using the parties' names).

How do we determine whether the parties achieve these ends? What tests will determine liability? How do the facts compare with the principles? How do the facts compare with similar facts in other cases?

How can the law be applied to the facts? What are the main issues to be discussed? How do the facts relate to the principles and issues that you have identified as important? Finally, has your written answer demonstrated your ability to consider and apply the law to this given facts situation?

WHAT NEXT?

You can see that it is important to stay focused during your exam, just as it was during your study time. In the next chapter, we will have a brief look at some factors that may interfere with your focus, and suggest some strategies to help you overcome these difficulties.

DEALING WITH PROBLEMS

> Past, and to come, seems best; things present, worst.
> Shakespeare, *Henry IV*, 1.3.108

Studying at university is about becoming (or at times at least behaving like) an adult. When you encounter problems, it is your responsibility to do something about them. There is a wide variety of help available at most campuses for all sorts of situations (health, finance, study problems...), but the staff who deal with these matters won't come to you. You need to identify what has gone wrong and look for solutions. In this chapter we'll outline some common study problems and give you starting points for dealing with them.

> Adversity is the first path to truth.
> Lord Byron, *Don Juan*, 12.50

'I think my tutor's hopeless'

One thing you must realise is that many tutors are postgraduate students who do some teaching as part of their research duties or to earn a little extra money. Unlike your school teachers, they have not dedicated their lives to teaching, and they often have very little experience. However, they do have a good knowledge of their subject and

DEALING WITH PROBLEMS

recent experience of being a university student, and they can share these with you. So perhaps you need to give your tutor a chance.

Take *positive* action. If the personality clash is causing real difficulties, you can try asking to change tutes, or you can wait a bit and see whether tutors change with the topics you are studying. You could also look on it as character building and good experience for the real world of law, remembering that you won't always get to work with people you like. If the person is really hopeless, go and see the lecturer or first year co-ordinator (phrasing your complaints in a polite and rational manner). You are now responsible for your own progress, and you should take action about problems that are affecting your learning and results.

'I broke my leg skiing/ had glandular fever/ caught a tropical disease and I'm really behind'

Student lifestyles seem to attract the influenza virus and other health disasters. The best solution is to make sure you pay attention to your diet, exercise and sleep. Although study is mainly a mental activity, you need a healthy body to let your mind work at its most efficient.

If you have been sick and had to miss classes, you can try some of these strategies:

- Don't get further behind—do THIS week's work before you think about revising all the bits you missed.
- Do your catching up backwards—don't worry if you don't understand it all. You can fill in the gaps later and just take it on trust until all the pieces fit together.
- Talk to someone about what you missed—half an hour's chat can be more useful than trying to decipher someone else's notes.
- If you're not feeling really well, don't force yourself to endlessly re-read long boring chapters. Do a little active work, small bits at a time.

- Let someone know—teaching staff and staff at the faculty office can't read your mind, especially if you're not there, so let them know about your health problems.
- See if you can, and, if you need to, apply for special consideration.

'I don't care about any of this any more'

It is not unusual to feel bored and lose motivation at some stage during your studies. Everybody gets bored with study and with putting the rest of their lives on hold while they complete their degree. For some people, a walk on the beach or a chocolate sundae will cure the problem, but for others it is not quite that easy to get fired up again.

We've talked a lot about study habits in Chapters 3 and 4. Many of these strategies can actually help to improve your motivation if you use them on a regular basis. So if you're feeling dull and listless about your study, why not try some of the following:

- set some clear short-term goals
- set yourself a time-frame
- reward yourself for completing tasks
- break your tasks into bite-sized pieces
- stop procrastinating—deal with the hard bits first
- refocus on the long view
- do some study with some friends
- don't make excuses—make progress.

Disasters come in all shapes and sizes. Try to put your problems in perspective—yes, it's awful to have the 'flu three times in one winter, but is that the same as being in hospital and rehab for six months? You need to tailor your reactions to the severity of the problem. Of course it seems bad to you, but how will other people view it?

DEALING WITH PROBLEMS

This is not to say that you won't get sympathy and support, but if you drop out of subjects every time something bad happens, you'll never finish your course. Don't make any hasty decisions without advice from people such as those we mentioned above, and remember that there is specific help available for many of the crises that occur in everyone's life. It may be that you need to drop some subjects, or go part time, or take a year off, but these are last resorts.

You'll find that all the active study strategies suggested in this book will make your study time more efficient, so even if you are having other problems in your life, you can still continue with your course. If you're feeling too upset to study, try to recognise that all the qualities that made you a good student or a good worker in the past still belong to you, and that you can access them. Don't let the feeling overwhelm you completely, but acknowledge that it's part of your life at the moment. You may find it helpful to make a list of strategies for yourself that you know have been valuable in the past. Concentrate on small achievable goals and reward yourself for reaching them.

'The exams just suddenly came along out of nowhere'

That sounds rather like Myth No. 2 right back in Chapter 3. The university year goes by very quickly. If you know you're in trouble, you can do something about it. If there were serious reasons which prevented you from studying earlier in the year, you must identify and follow up the procedures for special consideration. Most universities (and most faculties) have people who can help you with these sorts of problems. They may be called course advisers, mentors, peer tutors, learning skills advisers, counsellors, or some other title. As a first step, get in touch with these people and ask for help.

Don't waste your precious time by spending hours mentally berating yourself for all the things you haven't done. What is important now is to maximise your return from the limited time you have. You can still make use of all the active learning strategies we talked of earlier; you just have to do them in a more concentrated way.

Here are some other things you can do:

- Make a study timetable for the remaining time so you know that you can cover all you need to cover.
- Focus on the level of knowledge you need to get through each subject—this is no time for perfectionism.
- Make rational sacrifices: if there are things that you know you're never going to understand, don't waste time on them.
- Concentrate on improving your knowledge in areas where you've got a good basic grasp of what is happening (full marks on half the questions is a better return than 30% of everything).
- Don't stay up all night—the extra pages read overnight aren't worth the decrease in performance next day.

'My marks aren't up to standard'

These things happen. It is disappointing; the only thing to do is vow to learn from your mistakes. As a consolation, remember you are now studying at a higher level than you have done in the past. You are also surrounded by lots of similarly high-achieving students, so you may find it a bit of a shock to be getting average marks when you're used to being top of the class. Try to remember that although you're a pretty big fish, you're now in a rather large pond (see Chapter 2).

That being said, you can probably do better if you adjust your approach and study techniques to match the task more closely. Ask yourself some hard questions and answer them honestly:

- Are you doing regular study every day?
- Are you reviewing frequently?

DEALING WITH PROBLEMS

- Are you allowing adequate time for preparation?
- Are you studying actively (as opposed to doing 'desk time')?
- Are you making your study a priority?

If you are saying 'yes' to all of these, but you're still not achieving as well as you wish, then there are a couple of things to consider. First, if you persist, you will soon begin to consolidate your efforts. Also, you can learn from your present difficulties and improve your marks next semester. Another factor to think about is your motivation—are you in the right course? Maybe you're having problems because you're just not as interested in your subjects as you thought you would be.

'My family is really disappointed with my results'

This can be rather difficult, but in the last instance it's your life and it's up to you to decide your priorities. Some students find themselves in courses that don't really suit them. You may have chosen your course because of some family pressure, or because of an ideal image of studying law that doesn't match the reality of the daily grind. It may be that you're just finding out about how to function successfully at university; it may be that you have other issues to deal with; it may be that the other people don't understand exactly how hard study at this level is.

You have options about these pressures. You can try explaining to your family or friends what the situation really is. You can ask them to help you re-evaluate your goals. You can talk to someone who is totally neutral. If things are really bad, you may want to move out of home to try to establish yourself as an independent adult. If you really feel that you should live up to other people's expectations and you haven't been able to do so, try seeking extra help (from a learning skills adviser, or perhaps you could hire a private tutor) to ensure better results in the next semester.

STUDYING LAW AT UNIVERSITY

'I didn't pass'

You may not believe this now, but it's not the end of the world as we know it. It's not even necessarily the end of your course, or even that subject. Many successful graduates failed their first assignment; mostly that's because they were adjusting to university. More than a few successful lawyers have failed at least one subject during their undergraduate course (ask around—usually they're quite proud of it, thinking that they have somehow cheated the system). However, if you know you could have worked harder, then the solution to your problem is fairly clear. The time to worry is when the poor result is totally unexpected, and you can't see what to improve. Then you should consult a study skills adviser, your tutors or lecturers, or perhaps some later-year students to talk over the situation.

Know where you stand. Even if you know deep down that you didn't put enough study into the subject, it's still beneficial to look at your exam paper or ask for detailed feedback on your written assignments. It may be that you were not as hopeless as you believed—there are bound to be positive aspects to any assessment. Just as it's important to know what you don't know, it's also useful to see how much you have absorbed.

It is also valuable to see some examples of good answers, if your faculty has some to show you.

> There is nothing more stimulating than a case where everything goes against you.
> Sherlock Holmes in *The Hound of the Baskervilles*,
> Sir Arthur Conan Doyle

THE BOTTOM LINE

The main message is that nobody's study life is perfect. You can't plan for accidents, but if you make an effort to keep up throughout the year, then you will minimise the damage. Life as a student (or as a lawyer) doesn't consist of getting everything right first time: it is a process of continual development. All students, even at postgraduate level, continue to improve their study strategies and learn from past disappointments.

Part IV
CONCLUSION

FINAL REFLECTIONS ON LAW

> Happiness depends upon ourselves.
> Aristotle, 4th century BC, (translated by J.A.K. Thomson)

Your first year of studying law is unique, and every one of you will have different experiences, much as you will all bring different expectations to the course in the first instance. Your first year may end up teaching you more about university, and about yourself, than it teaches you about law. However, you will grow and learn in many ways. You may make decisions about whether or not you want to be a lawyer at all. You may develop a highly original overview of law and society (see Appendix IV). You may become set on a specific career within the law. On the other hand, you may just decide to see how things fall out in another couple of years.

> A jury consists of twelve persons chosen to decide who has the better lawyer.
> Robert Frost

STUDYING LAW AT UNIVERSITY

We have devised this book to aid your study and to help you tackle the mystique of the law. Demystifying the law will help you get a handle on the major concerns of your chosen field, and establishing good study habits early in your university career will help you make your way through both study and life in the law.

> As for the Future, your task is not to foresee, but to enable it.
> Antoine de Saint-Exupery (translated by S. Gilbert)

Remember that law can lead to all sorts of exciting and stimulating careers. Studying law will test both your intellect and your physical stamina, and we trust that this book will help you enjoy the experience.

APPENDIX I

SUGGESTIONS FOR FURTHER READING

Carven, J. 1994. *Understanding the Australian Legal System: a book for first time law students.* Law Book Company, Sydney

Clanchy, J. and Ballard, B. 1991. *Essay Writing for Students: a practical guide.* 2nd edition. Longman Cheshire, Melbourne

The CCH Macquarie Concise Dictionary of Modern Law. 1988. CCH Australia

Gawith, G. 1991. *Power learning: a student's guide to success.* Longman Cheshire, Melbourne

Krever, R. 1998. *Mastering Law Studies and Law Exam Techniques.* 4th edition. Butterworths Australia

Nygh, P. (ed.). 1998. *Butterworths Australian Legal Dictionary.* Butterworths Australia

'Melbourne University Law Review Style Guide' (in issues of the *Melbourne University Law Review*)

Murray-Smith, S. 1989. *Right words: a guide to English usage in Australia.* 2nd edition. Penguin

Osborn, P.G. 1993. *Osborn's Concise Law Dictionary.* 8th edition. L. Rutherford and S. Bone (eds). Sweet & Maxwell, London

Srivastava, D.K., Deklin, T. and Singh, P. 1995. *An Introduction to Australian Law.* Law Book Company, Sydney

Waller, L. 1995. *Derham, Maher and Waller: An Introduction to Law*. Law Book Company, Sydney

Williams, J.M. 1994. *Style: ten lessons in clarity & grace.* 4th edition. HarperCollins College Publishers

APPENDIX II

LEARNING STYLES QUIZ

For each of the following statements, rate yourself in order to discover your strengths and weaknesses. You probably will find that although you use strategies from all sections at some time or other, there will be one or two that stand out as your preferred learning modes. If things are spread pretty evenly, then maybe you are a well-balanced learner!

LEARNING STYLES

	Always	Sometimes	Never
Visuo-spatial			
I like to have my room organised so that all the things that go together stay together.	☐	☐	☐
I like to draw a map if someone is giving me directions.	☐	☐	☐
I like to make poster-style charts to study from.	☐	☐	☐
I use my hands or a drawing to help me describe complex things to other people.	☐	☐	☐

STUDYING LAW AT UNIVERSITY

	Always	Sometimes	Never
When I try to remember things, I can picture the page or the place I first saw them.	☐	☐	☐

Visuo-verbal

	Always	Sometimes	Never
I like to read over the instructions before I try something new.	☐	☐	☐
I like to rewrite things I have to learn.	☐	☐	☐
I like to make lists of things to do.	☐	☐	☐
I use lots of describing words when I'm explaining things to people.	☐	☐	☐
I like to take notes in complete sentences.	☐	☐	☐

Auditory

	Always	Sometimes	Never
I like to repeat instructions as I do new tasks.	☐	☐	☐
I prefer to listen to a story than to read the book.	☐	☐	☐
I like to talk over the lessons with some of my friends.	☐	☐	☐
I like people asking me questions so I can talk about what I've done or learned.	☐	☐	☐
I take point-form notes and don't like writing essays.	☐	☐	☐

Kinaesthetic

	Always	Sometimes	Never
I like to try something without bothering about the written instructions.	☐	☐	☐
I love taking things apart to see how they work.	☐	☐	☐

LEARNING STYLES QUIZ

	Always	Sometimes	Never
I like to make patterns of the things I have to learn.	☐	☐	☐
I'm good at practical tasks if people don't pester me.	☐	☐	☐
When I explain something, I use anything around me—knives and forks and sauce bottles—to show how the parts fit together.	☐	☐	☐

There is no 'right' or 'wrong' way to learn. You can use any mode to learn, but what you should consider is that some modes suit some types of learning better. For example, if you are studying for a practical exam, you should use some kinaesthetic methods: try doing the procedure without following written instructions; make sure you know how the parts fit together.

LEARNING TEMPERAMENTS

This little quiz is to help you identify your individual learning temperament. Once again, there are no right or wrong answers, and some sorts of information are more easily learned by those with one temperament or another. The best teachers enable students to approach the material from a multitude of directions; at tertiary level, you may need to organise this for yourself.

	Always	Sometimes	Never
The big picture learner			
Once I get an overview, the details fall into place.	☐	☐	☐

STUDYING LAW AT UNIVERSITY

	Always	Sometimes	Never
I like to get a feel for how the information fits together.	☐	☐	☐
I like to know what I'm meant to get out of a task before I start it.	☐	☐	☐
I like to look at the last page before I go back and read the rest of the book.	☐	☐	☐

The step-by-step learner

	Always	Sometimes	Never
I want to get each section right before I move on.	☐	☐	☐
I'm uncomfortable when new things happen really quickly.	☐	☐	☐
If I concentrate on the details and examples, I will work out the theory later.	☐	☐	☐
I like to see every episode of a TV series in order.	☐	☐	☐

The experiential learner

	Always	Sometimes	Never
I like to try out things for myself and test theories for myself.	☐	☐	☐
I tend to argue with people about how things work because I see them in my own way.	☐	☐	☐
I sometimes find that I discover things by myself.	☐	☐	☐
When I get a new computer game, I don't read the instructions, I just play and work it out as I go along.	☐	☐	☐

The collaborative learner

	Always	Sometimes	Never
I like talking over the lessons because other people can show me a different side of the information.	☐	☐	☐

LEARNING STYLES QUIZ

	Always	Sometimes	Never
I find that describing things to other people helps me to understand them myself.	☐	☐	☐
If I don't understand something, I'd rather ask someone about it than read a book.	☐	☐	☐
I can work quite well in a noisy environment.	☐	☐	☐

These short questionnaires are just starting points. If you are interested to find out more about yourself and your learning style, there are lots of online resources. Some of them even have long quizzes that you can do. A good starting place is 'The Keirsey Temperament Sorter <http://www.keirsey.com/cgi-bin-keirsey-newkts.cgi>. This page presents an online personality test you can do, and it gives detailed feedback about each personality type.

APPENDIX III

A STARTING POINT FOR USING WEB RESOURCES

LAW SITES

Law Professors on the Web
<http://www.butterworths.com.au>
This site has links to most Australian law faculties.

Washburn University School of Law
<http://lawlib.wuacc.edu/washlaw/>
This site has links to lots of good information such as law schools and libraries, bar exams (US), course materials, legal books, legal humour . . .

Butterworths Online
<http://www.butterworths.com.au>
Australia's largest legal database, with links to Australian resources, directories of lawyers, recent judgments, and a catalogue of recent law publications.

The Law Society Online
<http://lawsocnsw.asn.au/>
The home page of the NSW Law Society. It has useful links and daily media updates, information for the public and resources for lawyers.

NSW Young Lawyers can also be reached through the page above <http://lawsocnsw.asn.au/>. It has lots of good *information for students as well as regular updates on current issues in the courts.*

West's Legal Dictionary can be found at
<http://www.wld.com/>

Do I want to go to law school? This is the question asked at <http://www.baylor.edu> *You will find this a stimulating look at studying law.*

Learning Law, a page of general resources for the study of law, is located at
<http://www.law.umkc.edu/bgf-edu.htm#STUDENTS>

Gilbert Law Summaries Home Page
<http://www.gilbertlaw.com/>
Includes some fun items such as 'shark talk' and lawyer jokes, as well as good links to study advice and (US) law exams.

PERSONALITY AND LEARNING STYLES INFORMATION AND TESTS

Two good places to start are the page of IQ and Personality tests on the web:

http://www.keirsey.com/>

or you can try Yahoo! for some links

<http://www.yahoo.com/Science/Psychology/>

ONLINE HELP WITH WRITING AND STUDY

The Learning Skills Unit at the University of Melbourne
<http://www.services.unimelb.edu.au/lsu/>

The Learning Development Centre at the University of Western Sydney (Macarthur) <http://www.unilearning.net.au/>

STUDYING LAW AT UNIVERSITY

The Study Strategies homepage has some good advice for law students at <http://www.d.umn.edu/student/loon/acad/strat/>

ONLINE CITATION GUIDELINES

An introduction to basic legal citation can be found at <http://www.law.cornell.edu>

A good starting web site for general referencing guidelines is <http://www.ddce.cqu.edu.au/refandcitation/home.htm>

A site with a lot more detail and links to other resources: Louisiana State University 'How to Cite the Internet' <http://www.lsu.edu/guests/poli/public_html/lis.html>

APPENDIX IV

THE VIEW FROM THE KITCHEN

Studying a law degree is a lot like peeling an onion. From the outside it looks a little dry and unappetising, but nicely symmetrical and ultimately nourishing. When you start peeling layers, however, it becomes obvious that the apparent symmetry is merely the result of years of repetition, covering itself with the same insubstantial film year after year. If you stop at this point, you depart cynical, misty-eyed, but still faithful that there is some logic that you haven't quite grasped. However, if you go further you gradually acclimatise to the vapours that used to moisten your eyes, and become so used to the process of peeling that you don't pause to think what you'll find when the last layer is gone, or what you will do if there is no 'last' layer—if there is nothing but layers.

For some, the idea of being paid to peel these layers is abhorrent, so they start dicing from the outset. Lightly stir-fry the pieces of the law in a wok, add some chopped capsicum, some basil, an egg, salt and pepper to taste and you have a theory of law—not very much like the original article but far more palatable. You needn't sacrifice your principles and you can be objective because, by frying the onion, you won't be affected by the vapours that seem to blur everyone else's vision.

Others reject the onion entirely, looking for alternatives

among the greengrocers of society. Some opt for the designer avocado with its tough but fair core—a far more nutritious fruit, but not everyone can afford them. Some look to the multi-centred pomegranate with its even distribution of red pulp and seeds—but few people have seen one close up and others appear to have abandoned them because they failed as a cash crop. A third group have taken the debate to a new level: after the so-called 'Tomato School' suffered a schism over a bitter debate as to whether it should be included as a fruit or a vegetable, the agricultural and horticultural schools were spawned and their arguments fill many pages of the leading periodicals.

In the final analysis, whether you enjoy a Waldorf salad, a banana split or just hoeing into half a pound of red meat, the most important thing for most law students is to pass and get a job. In doing so, however, it is very easy to ignore the fact that you are making decisions and assumptions that change your perception of what the law is and what it should be. Yet law, perhaps more than any other degree, has the capacity to empower the men and women who study it. This empowerment can be used to take advantage of the world in which we live, or to right many of the more obvious wrongs within society. But the latter objective is served no better by dark grey suits who claim to be merely doing their jobs than it is by academics who write critiques to other like-minded academics without so much as rippling the status quo.

It may well be naive to presume that all lawyers should consider themselves social workers, but it is far from unreasonable to expect them to be honest about what motivates them and realistic about what they hope to achieve. This applies equally to those within the law school who base their degrees around meeting the right people over cocktails and getting employed at one of the larger corporate machines, as it does to those who spend their time writing indecipherable essays about allegorical metaphysical self-referential fruit salads.

THE VIEW FROM THE KITCHEN

The message of all this is not that earning gold bullion for ruining people's lives is evil. Nor is it that sticking by your principles in the face of reality is a waste of time. Rather, the message is that you should at least consider why you're studying law, what you want to do with it, and whether that reason and that future will fulfil all your dietary and spiritual needs in the years to come.

Simon Chesterman
reprinted from *Purely Dicta* (April 1993)